A GUIDE
FOR WALL-WATCHERS

Don't know what to put on your walls?
Not quite pleased with what's there now?
Time to relax and make wall decorating
the fun it should be.

Let this helpful guide show you the
way to make your rooms more imaginative, unusual and exciting—and save
you time and money, too.

all about walls

by John Elmo, A.I.D.

Illustrated by Joseph Bertelli

POPULAR LIBRARY · NEW YORK

CONTENTS

ABOUT THE COVER 8

LIST OF ILLUSTRATIONS 10

PREFACE 11

PART ONE: HOW TO MAKE WALLS
             EXCITING 13

The importance of walls . . .
what are accessories and their
function . . . nine basic pointers for good wall arrangement.

PART TWO: HOW TO PLAN A WALL
             ARRANGEMENT 23

Techniques in wall arrangement
. . . scale . . . balance . . . unity
. . . pointers on pictures . . .
mirror magic . . . the third dimension . . . coordinating furniture and wall accessories . . .
plan your room on paper . . .
correct way to hang wall objects.

PART THREE: UNCOMMON SOLUTIONS
            TO COMMON PROBLEMS .. 53

30 sketches showing how wall-
decorating problems are solved
with proper accessories in living
rooms . . . dens and family
rooms . . . dining and breakfast

rooms . . . bedrooms . . . kitchens and bathrooms.

PART FOUR: WHERE TO FIND GOOD
             ACCESSORIES   95

Local stores have fine interior
design services . . . mix accessories with period styles
. . . use travel souvenirs . . .
charming outdoor accessories
. . . seasonal accessories . . .
use of plants and hobby collections . . . make your own
accessories . . . how to budget
your accessories dollars.

PART FIVE: THE WORLD OF COLOR . . 107

Get the most out of color . . .
use color to freshen a room . . .
psychology of color . . . six
ways to find inspiration . . .
choosing colorful accessories
. . . color scheme variations
. . . lighting effects . . . creating illusions with color . . .
glossary of color terms.

PART SIX: SHEDDING LIGHT ON
             WALL ART 127

Various rooms require different
lighting . . . special lighting effects for wall accessories . . .
wall-washers . . . cornice lighting . . . strip lighting . . . spot-
lights.

PART SEVEN: POPULAR STYLES IN FUR-
NITURE AND ACCESSO-
RIES 135

Blend decorating styles . . . accessorizing in the traditional
style . . . accessorizing provincial settings . . . contemporary
accessorizing . . . guide to
home-furnishings styles . . . traditional eighteenth-century English . . . French traditional furniture . . . American traditional
styles . . . French Provincial
. . . Mediterranean . . . contemporary . . . Modern.

GLOSSARY OF DECORATIVE MOTIFS 168

GLOSSARY 171

INDEX 179

ABOUT THE COVER

The cover picture illustrates six basic accessorizing ideas. How many of them can you spot?

1. *Use of pictures*—the collection of pen-and-ink figure drawings all framed uniquely.
2. *Dimensional accessories*—the superb nine-arm Spanish candled sconce.
3. *Hobbies*—a group of ceramic pottery clustered together.
4. *Decorative pillows*—together with the ottoman used for comfort and color interest.
5. *Living plants*—a collection of hanging pots grouped together.
6. *Accent tables*—used here as coffee and chair-side tables.

All of these accessorizing ideas will be studied in the pages that follow.

LIST OF ILLUSTRATIONS

Cover 8
Elements of scale, balance, and unity 26, 29, 31
Elements of grouping 42
Floor plans 44
Hints for hanging 48–49
Room settings: Living rooms 56–64
    Dens and family rooms 65–72
    Dining and breakfast rooms 81–84
    Bedrooms 85–90
    Kitchens and bathrooms 91–93
Varieties in lighting 132
Queen Anne 143
Chippendale 145
Hepplewhite and Sheraton 147
Adam 149
Louis XIV 151
Louis XV 152
Louis XVI 153
Directoire and Empire 155
Colonial 157
Post-Revolution Federal 159
Early-American 161
French Provincial 163
Mediterranean 165
Contemporary 167
Glossary of decorative motifs 168–169

PREFACE

What is a wall? A wall is a boundary. A keeping out, or a keeping in, of something wonderful—dependent upon your momentary thoughts, and your personal view of life. We put things on walls to draw attention to this boundary or to negate its existence. It's as simple as that. What we do with our walls reveals our likes and dislikes, just as our way of dressing reveals our personality.

Man has attended to walls from earliest habitable times. First, by decorating them with hand-scratched scenes of his activities; then, with added sophistication, giving the designs dimension by carving them. When man became mobile and moved to other locations, the desire to carry possessions developed into the practice of hanging familiar objects. This is still something we enjoy doing today! How easy it is to feel comfortable in a strange new house, simply by hanging pictures or accessories that we enjoyed seeing in a previous home.

There really isn't any proper way to treat a wall, just as there isn't any proper way to arrange a room. Any number of variations can be correct. What becomes "proper" is guided by three points: personality, budget, and good taste. Keeping these elements in mind will insure good decorating results.

Attention should be paid to all walls, and care should be taken in selecting wall decorations. Don't be afraid of using items that have a personal meaning, that give you the pleasure of past related experiences; they can really help transform a house into a home.

Where to start? How to start? Well, first know what you want to do with the room. Second, ask yourself how many walls do you want to decorate? How are they related to each other? How will the eye move? Will it be a pleasing flow; an easy movement? Before deciding on color or method of grouping, however, there is one obvious point that is often overlooked: Start with clean walls. How terrible any object will look on a wall if the surrounding areas are dirty!

It's true that walls may be difficult to handle, but since they're there as boundaries, let's be creative with them. It takes time and patience arranging all component parts to form a unified whole, but it's well worth the effort. The end result will surely be rooms for enjoyment.

                                            John Elmo, A.I.D.

PART ONE

HOW TO
MAKE WALLS EXCITING

PART ONE
HOW TO
MAKE WALLS EXCITING

Wall decorating can be an adventure that is one of the most rewarding creative challenges you've ever experienced.

Today's way of life calls for an individual approach to furnishing a home, and walls are excellent areas one can decorate to best express personal tastes. By virtue of the vast amount of space walls occupy, they are important and deserving of the very best choice one can give to wall accessories.

SEEING A ROOM FROM ALL SIDES

When you first enter a room, your eye wanders neither up nor down, but straight ahead, and what else do you see but wall space?

Since walls are often the first thing people notice when they walk into a room, the easiest and often the most inexpensive way to set the decorating tone of your home is by carefully choosing and planning your wall decor to fit within your overall decorating scheme.

Even though you may have arranged the furniture and curtained the windows, until you have dressed the walls a room is still incomplete. You have probably had the experience of visiting a home where there seemed to be a bare, unfinished appearance. The reason may well have been that the owner dismissed the walls with no greater imagination than a coat of paint and a few scattered pictures placed haphazardly.

Today, with so many beautiful accessories available, there's no reason why all your interiors can't be a constant source of pleasure and visual excitement from floor to ceiling.

WHAT IS AN ACCESSORY?

The word "accessory" is a rather flexible term that applies to all the incidental objects that complete a room. Accessories are the cosmetics applied to a room that reveal your personal fancy. They supply the many little, extra comforts and conveniences that make a house a warm and cheerful home.

As long as they add to the beauty of a room, accessories can be useful or not. Items like clocks, mirrors, ashtrays, throw pillows, cigarette lighters, and small card-holding boxes justify their existence for practical as well as decorative purposes.

But it's also nice to know that there is an area of decorating where you needn't be thinking about function all the time. When you find an accessory that is utterly useless, but irresistible because it has the right colors or design feeling to fit into a certain spot in your home, give in to your impulse. Buy it for the sheer pleasure it will give you.

When you want to know what to buy or whether the accessories you now have are suitable, just ask yourself this question: What are they doing to improve the room? To help decoratively, an accessory should add one or more of these ingredients:

Color. If an accessory does no more than supply a dash of accent color where needed, it belongs. The crisp, bright pillows against a neutral sofa fabric, the colorful painting used over a fireplace, the polychrome plaques that repeat all the colors in the room—all these contribute to the look of coordination a room needs.

Texture. Excitement walks in the door where textural contrast is present. A room that has wood furniture or wood-paneled walls needs the textured relief of polished silver, brass, chrome, or mirrors, as well as the textural differences found in smooth and rough fabrics. Much of this contrast can also come from accessories.

Form. Rooms are made up of different shapes and lines—round, rectangular, oblong, curved, horizontal, or vertical. Accessories help to make a room interesting when they add variety to these forms. A correctly scaled vertical picture is a good accent over a horizontal chest; while round, oval, and hexagonal shapes are nice contrasts when used over a long, rectangular sofa.

Balance. Even when furniture is correctly distributed around the room so that all the weight is not at one end, there is something missing until wall accessories are put into place to balance the weight from floor to ceiling. Suppose you have a breakfront on one wall, and a long, low buffet on the opposite wall. Accessories over the buffet, in order to do their job,

should be fairly substantial in size and bulk to balance
the effect of the towering breakfront.

CREATE YOUR OWN DECORATING OUTLOOK

Accessories are fun to work with because there are
so many kinds of objects to choose from and dozens
of different ways to group them together. When you
buy a sofa or chair, it's the furniture designer who
has done the creative work, leaving you with little
more to do than to put his design into place.

How the picture changes when you get down to
the exciting job of creating a wall arrangement! You
are literally starting with a clean slate—a bare stretch
of wall space covered in most cases with a coat of
white, neutral, or pastel paint. The rest is up to you.
Here is a chance to really let your imagination go and
express your true taste and personality through the
decorative objects you bring together.

While some people rely on clichés in wall arrangement, merely putting together a few pictures or hanging a mirror, there's no need for you to follow suit.

The more you learn about accessories and how to
arrange them, the more you will be able to shed the old
"safe-but-dull" strategy that so many people resort
to when putting the finishing touches to their interiors.

NINE BASIC POINTERS ON GOOD WALL ARRANGEMENT

In decorating with wall accessories, success is a
matter of remembering a few techniques that aren't
difficult at all to master. Below are nine points you
should know about in order to create better-looking

walls. If you do nothing more than read this list and keep it in mind, you are bound to get good decorating results.

1. Hang accessories at the right level. For some reason, many people tend to place accessories too high on the wall. This is displeasing because it forces the eye to wander upward and in most cases it destroys the unity that should exist between furniture and wall decor. Throughout this book you will see illustrations of accessories grouped at the proper height to give an overall feeling of harmony and balance to the entire room. Study the placements.

2. Leave enough space between items. When objects crowd each other, none of them is shown off to its best advantage. Spacing too far apart, on the other hand, creates displeasing bare spots on the wall and breaks the unity and flow of the pattern you are trying to create. Allow a moderate amount of space between accessories—a little more for larger objects, a little less for smaller ones.

3. Use accessories in keeping with the quality of your other possessions. If you've splurged on a beautiful sofa or have a handsome cabinet you are proud to own, make the most of these treasures by choosing suitable companion accessories. A diamond needs the right setting to really show off its sparkle.

4. Include all the walls in your decorating plan. Just as furniture should be well distributed around a room for a look of careful balance, so should a grouping of accessories on one wall be complemented by some additional "weight" on the other walls. It's good to have one outstanding wall as a focal point for the room, but do reserve some of your pretty things to use on the other walls.

5. Decorate every room in the house. You will find

that the visual areas in a small house or apartment seem to increase when there is something to stop and admire at every turn. Particularly important in livening up the overall appeal of your home are the finishing touches applied to the halls, foyer, stairway, and other areas that are usually neglected. Even the kitchen and bathrooms can be made more interesting with the addition of unconventional accessories—pictures, plaques, or sconces. Still lifes, botany prints, and other pictures, framed in glass to protect them from steam and cooking grease, help alleviate the all-work-and-no-play aspect of a kitchen. A pair of wall sconces, a planter, or some scenic pictures create a luxurious atmosphere in the plainest of bathrooms. In a foyer too small for furniture, three-dimensional wall accessories give meaning to what otherwise may seem like wasted space.

6. *Use just enough accessories to achieve a finished look.* A woman's costume often improves when she removes a piece of jewelry or snips off the flower that came with the dress. The same can be said for rooms. There's no need to clutter up every piece of furniture with small objects like ashtrays, boxes, and bric-a-brac, particularly if the surface itself has a marble, inlaid, or other decorative top. The beauty of emphasizing wall accessories is that they give a room that desirable lived-in look.

7. *When using smaller objects, link them together with a theme.* Collections of interesting items have a more orderly look than a hodgepodge. Instead of one paperweight, an ashtray, and a figurine, try grouping three or four different kinds of paperweights. Clusters of small boxes, candle holders, or decorative bottles in different shapes and sizes combine attractively.

8. *Use three-dimensional accessories.* Pictures are indispensable as a means of bringing warmth, charm,

color, and artistic beauty into the home—but don't rely on them entirely. Contrast is effective in stepping up the tempo of a decorating scheme. On your walls, contrast means using the interestingly shaped mirrors, clocks, sconces, plaques, and other objects that do so much to enliven a room.

9. *Do something different.* A true opportunity to be different comes when you start accessorizing, so try something that's out of the ordinary. You don't have to hang a mirror over the dresser just because you've always seen it done that way. Why not pictures, sconces, or perhaps a smaller mirror combined with other objects? Over the mantel, make your choice a mirror, clock, or unusual plaque, instead of the usual picture. The plaque might be a free-form sculpture— perhaps a rambling branch with colorful blossoms. Unique ideas may not come readily at first, but as you leaf through the pages of this book, you will find illustrations to stir your imagination.

PART TWO

HOW TO
PLAN A WALL ARRANGEMENT

PART TWO

HOW TO
PLAN A WALL ARRANGEMENT

Think about the most successful dinner party you ever gave, when guests raved about the meal and your husband beamed with approval.

Didn't it all begin with that sudden impulse to put the cookbook aside for a moment and add your own variations?

You can do the same with decorating—achieving far more spectacular results. It's that extra bit of spice you add that will make your home unique.

Any wall arrangement chosen would be bland if you merely adhered to a set of rules and added no sparkle of your own. There are, however, certain basic facts you should be aware of in order to artistically group decorative objects. By understanding the rules, and by allowing yourself freedom of self-expression, you can arrive at the happy medium that lies between being too rigid or too flexible.

TECHNIQUES IN WALL ARRANGEMENT

Wall arrangements that excite the senses are made up of objects in the right *scale*, put together to achieve

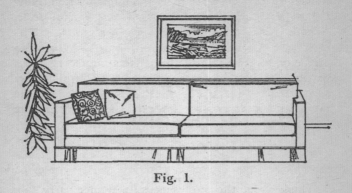

Fig. 1.

Fig. 2.

proper *balance*. The result has a *unity* and flow of movement that we refer to as good composition. Now let us take a closer look at these key words—*scale*, *balance*, and *unity*—to see what they mean.

Scale is the relationship of all items in a room to one another. The size of the objects you select for a particular wall arrangement should be determined by such considerations as the dimensions of the room, the size of the wall you are covering, and the furniture proportions within the room.

What is correct scale for a particular setting can be a choice of alternative arrangements. Over a sofa, for example, either of these two selections would be equally correct:

1. A single large picture. Provided it does not seem to overwhelm the sofa and is in proper scale, as shown in Figure 1.

2. A grouping of several smaller objects. Figure 2 shows this arrangement. Together, the pictures and clock are massive enough in scale to look correct when placed over a large piece of furniture. If you used only a few pictures and removed the other object, the grouping would become insignificant and would result in what is called a "postage-stamp" effect.

Balance, as discussed previously, refers to the proper weight distribution between a combination of objects. When there's a flowing rhythm to items grouped together, the result is pleasing to a person's eye movement.

Choose either symmetrical or asymmetrical balance. Symmetrical or formal balance is the placement of even patterns. Figure 3 shows formal balance—a sofa balanced on either end by lamps and end tables, with a painting flanked by plaques centered over the sofa.

The next figure shows an asymmetrical or informal

arrangement—a lamp and table at one end, a large
picture with a wall light at the other end, and a
plaque placed off-center above the sofa. While either
is proper, formal balance is easier for most people to
plan without professional help and is best suited to
formal, traditional rooms. Correct anywhere when
properly done, informal balance is a young and fresh
approach that has particular merit in contemporary
settings that call for dramatic impact.

Unity, or good composition, is a term used by artists
and photographers and refers to the grouping of objects so that no one object overwhelms the others and
each seems correct and belongs. Unity can be achieved
by using a set of similar objects, such as a group of
botany prints with matching frames, or a mirror having
identical sconces. Unity can also be achieved with objects that vary in size, shape, and texture, as shown in
Figures 5 and 6. Items are placed fairly close together
so that the eye can move smoothly from one to the
other.

After you have grasped the essentials of scale, balance, and unity, you can proceed with confidence to
the really creative part of planning wall arrangements.

POINTERS ON PICTURES

Of all the items that can be labeled accessories, pictures are the most widely used in homes, because they
usually are colorful and give interest whether used
singly, or in combination with other decorative objects.

Choose the right frame. Pictures that are light in
feeling—pastels, black and white sketches, simple drawings—require simple frames. You can use bolder,
carved frames when dealing with traditional oils or
other subjects that carry a heavier "weight." Crisp

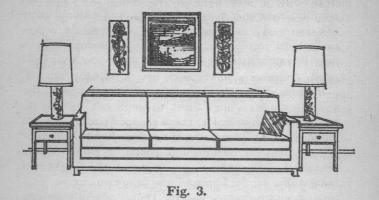

Fig. 3.

Fig. 4.

modern art looks best framed simply with no added embellishment. Matting makes small or delicate pictures appear larger and more impressive, and colored mats offer an easy, inexpensive way to coordinate accessories with other room colors. One should always bear in mind that the picture is what you want noticed. A frame should never overpower the subject.

Pictures attract the eye when they contrast with the wall, so choose your frames to stand out against the background paint color, the wallpaper pattern, or the wood paneling. Generally, the frame should be darker in tone than the background. Metal or gilded frames provide a nice contrast against wood paneling. On a busy wallpaper background, the subject matter of pictures should be simple and the frame carefully chosen to give delineation.

Develop variety in your groupings. Charming effects can be achieved by combining pictures of different styles and subjects.

THE MAGIC OF MIRRORS

Functional as well as attractive, mirrors are always popular and can be an excellent way of achieving special effects in decorating.

Choose the correct size. A mirror should be large enough to reflect the head and shoulders and should be hung at eye level for a standing person. Hang console shelves, teamed with mirrors, about thirty-three to thirty-six inches above the floor. Small mirrors, unless placed on a narrow wall, belong in groupings with other objects.

Think about reflections. A well-positioned mirror can double the effectiveness of an attractive accessory on the opposite wall by casting its reflection. Con-

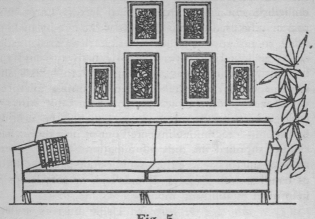

Fig. 5.

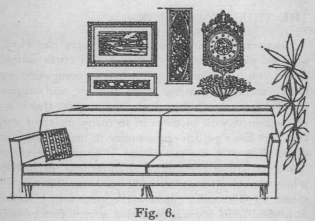

Fig. 6.

versely, you should not place a mirror where it repeats the image of a room's architectural defects. Large mirrors may be used effectively to fool the eye by making small rooms appear larger—a trick that works especially well in tiny foyers, narrow hallways, and the diminutive dining areas of many modern houses and apartments. A dining table placed against a mirrored wall, for example, doubles the size of the table. Mirrors can also be skillfully employed to enhance the lighting in a room—a technique invented out of necessity when candles supplied the only illumination. Today, placement of mirrors where they will bounce back the light of candles, wall sconces, chandeliers, or soft lamps is helpful in establishing mood.

Try a montage of mirrors. Using mirrors collectively is an intriguing way to decorate a wall. Choose different shapes, sizes, and frames for the best and most interesting effect.

THE THIRD DIMENSION

Discover the third dimension—objects like clocks, sconces, planters, plaques, shelves, and curio cabinets —and you have the real secret behind composing wall arrangements of genuine depth, interest, and originality. Tridimensional objects may be used by themselves or combined with pictures in so many different ways that here lies a golden opportunity to make your home come alive with the excitement of genuine creativity.

Objects placed together complement each other when there are variations in finishes and textures. The gleam of a metallic finish—a copper-toned rooster, burnished-brass sconce, or gilded mirror frame—often gives just the effect you need to brighten a wall of wood-toned picture frames. Never use more than one

Disarmingly simple, this serene study corner develops charm from the accessories easily found in gift shops and country stores. The framed prints are reproductions of old advertisements. For the one important accessory every grouping should have, Syroco's authentic reproduction of the Crested American eagle is the perfect choice because it adds a three-dimensional quality to the barn-siding walls.

As featured in *Family Circle*

A study in perfect symmetry, this butternut-paneled wall becomes a dramatic focal point for an elegantly dressed living room. The valance, shaped to repeat the sofa curves, helps form a niche for this important piece of furniture and becomes a framework for the autumn-colored Syroco Floral-Mates arrangement.

A great big welcome is the feeling established right at the front door in this apartment entrance. Adding to the stylized wallpaper and needlepoint rug, are the country provincial mirror and console table. The yellow tulips provide the necessary color accent.

Opposite: Forever fresh and exciting, red, white and blue gives a contemporary look to an eighteenth-century dining room. Perfectly at home with English furniture adaptations is the most important accessory in the room—Syroco's reproduction of an authentic Louis XV nine-arm sconce.

Against a wall of orange silk paper, black and white prints teamed with a Saxony five-arm sconce and figurines in distressed walnut finish are a superb understatement. Note the pleasant, informal balance achieved with rather formal pieces by using two different picture frames and by placing one figurine slightly above the other. The grouping is not static.

A small hallway becomes a grand entrance when the walls are emphasized to compensate for lack of floor space. A sophisticated ensemble, the rich Florentine wall mirror and pair of three-arm sconces above a slender marble-topped table provide both function and eye appeal without interfering with the flow of traffic.

Like the prologue of a play, a front hall should prepare the visitor fo
what lies ahead. Unmistakably, this foyer sets the scene for a hearty
atmosphere with strong Mediterranean overtones. Wall accessories, with
a sixteenth-century Spanish look, are appropriately outlined by heavy
wood beams. The brass and leather covered chest is a perfect receptacle
for magazines and papers.

Opposite: A burst of summer color enters the dining room with these
baskets brimming with fruits and flowers. Part of a collection of stun-
ning paint-it-yourself plaques, what better way to express yourself and
your creativity? By following the simple steps it's easy to achieve the
desired professional look.

In this remodeled basement playroom, the wood floor is hand-painted to simulate wood grain. The lightweight foam beams give the room increased height; the over-scaled fireplace opening has been changed to a half-round and made smaller. Nineteenth-century carpenter tools complement the delightful, authentic Syroco decoys.

In a room with masculine overtones, traditional pictures in simple frames add to a feeling of quiet luxury. The accent pedestal table, from a collection by Syroco, echoes the green fireplace trim. The clay tile floor and zebra-skin rug reinforce the masculine scheme.

metallic finish in the same setting; few metallic finishes look well together.

Since picture and mirror frames are generally limited to definite shapes, take advantage of the change of pace possible with the freer forms of three-dimensional wall objects. Fighting game cocks with sweeping tails, baskets of fruit and flowers, horns of plenty, floral sprays, or leaf-and-branch plaques—all of these dispel the monotony of conventional shapes and sizes.

Bring a sense of order to your effects. While variation in shape and size is always welcome, there must be some planning and sense of harmony to the completed grouping. This can best be explained by studying the figures on page 42, where in each case there is a unifying element making free-form wall hangings effective. In one example, similar birds-on-the-wing fly in formation; in another, four floral plaques are evenly spaced; and the third shows a simple, oblong mirror chosen as the nucleus of an array of figurines.

COORDINATING FURNITURE AND WALL ACCESSORIES

Since many of your accessories will be grouped around furniture rather than on isolated walls, it is helpful to know the rules for coordinating these two elements.

The sofa, end table, and lamp grouping. Hang your accessories low enough over the sofa to form a unified grouping, yet high enough so guests will not hit against them when leaning back. If table lamps are at both ends, confine your accessories to the sofa area.

Mantels. Since a mantel is often a room's focal point, reserve your best accessories for this area. A single,

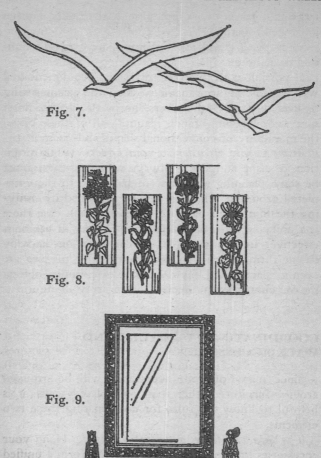

Fig. 7.

Fig. 8.

Fig. 9.

large picture or eye-stopping three-dimensional piece is often the most effective choice. Avoid detracting from the wall item with a profusion of bric-a-brac on the mantel shelf.

Headboards. Center your arrangement over the bed with the lowest piece above the head of a person sitting up. Include wall lights if you wish to dispense with night-table lights.

Built-in wall units. Using only books can be monotonous when you have a long wall of built-in furniture and shelving. Seek variety by hanging a few pictures or plaques within the unit. Pictures need not always be wall-hung—stand them up against shelves occasionally for a varied look.

Stairwells. Here is one of the few places you can stagger wall objects diagonally without the undesirable effect of moving the eye on a meaningless tangent. Pictures and other flat objects are preferable, unless the staircase is unusually wide.

For a pleasing balance between furniture and wall accessories, plan for an occasional vertical arrangement to alternate with the horizontal look of furniture. An oblong picture hung over a sofa, or a row of pictures hung vertically, introduces a freshness to the overall feeling. If all furniture in the room is rectangular, one or two oval or round accessories would be an interesting choice.

WORK IT OUT ON PAPER FIRST

Once you've learned the rules, going at it hammer-and-nails may seem like the quickest way to get pictures and other accessories on the walls, but it's far more efficient to set your tool kit aside for a moment and first work with pencil and paper.

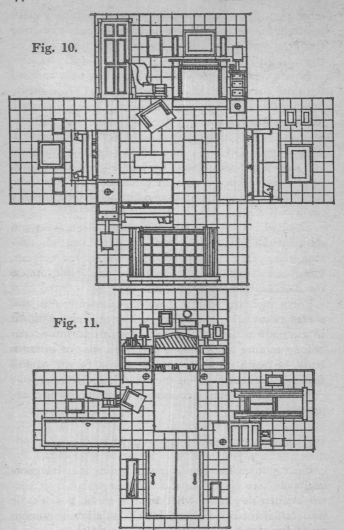

Fig. 10.

Fig. 11.

All your planning should be done from a paper-and-pencil sketch that includes the floor and the four walls. See figures on page 44.

Because all objects in a room are interrelated, the most effective wall arrangements start with the best floor plans. Accessories seem to fall into place much more easily and naturally when the furniture is well positioned according to good decorating and maximum livability. The first step, therefore, is to work out a floor plan, then create your various wall arrangements.

1. After measuring the room, draw an outline on graph paper, using a scale of one inch to one foot. Next show the locations of doors, windows, any obstructions, and electrical outlet placements. Now place four additional sheets of graph paper, to represent the walls, around the first, and indicate on these the height of your ceiling.

2. Draw scale plans of the furniture to be used in the room, using the same ratio of one inch to one foot. Keep your drawing simple, showing just the outline of each piece. At the same time, draw outlines of mirrors, clocks, pictures, and other major wall accessories you plan to use. Cut out the models and you are ready to begin experimenting with possible floor and wall plans.

3. With the furniture spread in miniature before you, start by placing the most important pieces. In a living room, this would be the main seating group; in the dining room the table and chairs; in the bedroom, bed and night tables. Once you have found the best possible spot for basics, the rest will fall into place easily.

4. When you have what appears to be a workable plan, test it for practicality. Have you allowed enough space for doors to swing open and shut? Is there a

free flow of traffic around furniture? Is the television set placed where it may be viewed by everyone without moving chairs? Have you avoided placing furniture too close to air-conditioning or heating units? Are there enough lamps and other lighting fixtures for reading and other activities and are there occasional tables for ashtrays, and snacking? Visualize yourself and other members of the family living in the room and going about their normal routines. This will help to anticipate all your needs and iron out any problems in advance.

5. Study your floor plan from an aesthetic viewpoint. Scale and balance are important points to consider if a room arrangement is to please the eye. Unless your furniture is properly scaled and balanced, you will have great difficulty later in working with suitable wall-accessory arrangements. A king-size bed, massive breakfront, or huge sofa are wrong for rooms of smaller than average size. Also incorrect is the use of massive and dainty furniture in the same setting—the dainty slipper chair next to a baby-grand piano, the diminutive coffee table centered on a long sofa, or the man-sized lounge chair dwarfing a petite period sofa. Bear in mind that "weight" can be visual as well as physical—dark-wood finishes or deep-colored fabrics make furniture appear heavier, while blond tones or pale fabrics give it lightness.

6. On each scale model of a wall, draw in the height of the furniture, windows, and doors indicated on the centered floor plan. A study of this elevation drawing will enable you to decide whether or not your furniture seems correct against the wall. Study will also determine how much bare wall space is available for planning accessory groupings. Consider the furniture plan first. If there are too many different heights, giv-

ing the illusion of the Manhattan skyline, the room will be jumpy.

7. Working with one wall at a time, arrange your scale-model accessories over the mantel, sofa, headboard, buffet, or whatever. When you have arrived at a pleasing arrangement, paste down or trace your models onto the elevation drawing. Look at it with a critical eye. If the accessories you have chosen are too small for the surrounding furniture, you will detect the forementioned "postage-stamp" look. If they are too large, they will make the wall overpower the furniture. If they are just right, you will see the arrangement as a pleasing picture, with all the objects blending into a harmonious unit.

8. As a final and highly effective method of checking your wall plan, place all accessories on the floor in front of the wall where you expect to hang them. Arrange them as indicated on your elevation sketch. Stand back and you can visualize the objects as they will appear on the wall. Now is the time to make any changes or try out alternate arrangements that come to mind. When you are convinced you have the right feeling, grab your tools and commence hanging.

GETTING THE HANG OF IT

It's easy to hang any object if you know what your walls are made of, which type hardware is required, and what tools to use. Pictures, mirrors, shelves, and other wall-hung objects vary greatly in weight and may have to be hung on a variety of surfaces—and the technique that works for a small, lightweight picture on a plaster wall will not secure a fifty-pound mirror to a background of brick.

If you are hanging pictures, mirrors, and other ob-

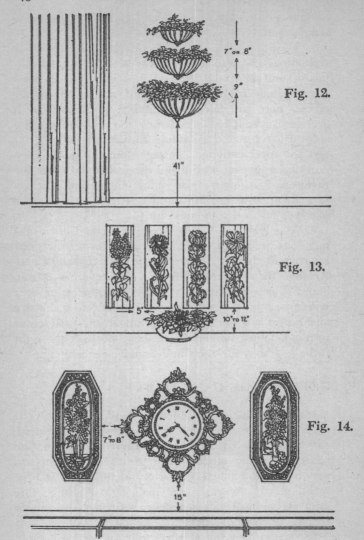

Fig. 12.

Fig. 13.

Fig. 14.

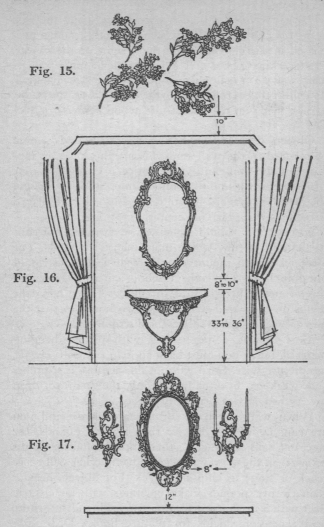

Fig. 15.

10"

Fig. 16.

8" to 10"

33" to 36"

Fig. 17.

8"

12"

jects that weigh less than twenty pounds, and the wall is plaster or sheet rock, use angled picture hooks purchased in the right size for the weight of the object. Plaster chips easily, and it is best to hammer gently, using a piece of cellophane tape as a protective backing. The procedure for wood-paneled walls is the same, except that you may substitute wood screws for picture hooks.

Objects weighing more than twenty pounds should be secured to the wall studs. Locate the studs by rapping on the wall until you notice a change in tone from a hollow sound to a solid thump. Studs are behind the area that has a solid sound and usually are placed sixteen inches apart on center.

Special care should be taken in hanging mirrors, particularly if they weigh more than ten pounds. The ideal way is to mount on the wall a wood strip of one-fourth-by-four-inch plywood, cut to a size about three-fourths the width of the mirror. Then hang the hooks on the wood strip, using two hooks so that the mirror will have better weight distribution.

Most objects come backed with proper hanging material, but if you must back an item yourself, always use picture wire. Cord will not do, because it stretches and weakens, eventually causing the item to drop lower than it was originally placed.

When walls are brick or other masonry and you are hanging objects lighter than twenty pounds, use steel-cut nails, hammering them into the mortar points rather than the masonry, because hammering will cause brick or stone to chip and crack. For objects heavier than twenty pounds make openings with an electric drill with a masonry drill or a star drill, and substitute lead expansion shields for picture hooks. Drill right into the brick or stone.

Tile walls or brick walls that have been covered over by plaster also require the drilling procedure described above, whether the object weighs more or less than twenty pounds.

Shelves with metal-bracket arm supports can be hung in two ways. It is best to secure the strips directly to the studs with wood screws. When a shelf must be hung in a certain spot where there is no stud, use toggle bolts if the wall is plaster and Molly bolts if the wall is sheet rock. For wood paneling, self-threading screws are necessary. For small, lightweight shelves that will support only small, light objects, self-threading screws that are one and one-half inches or longer will do the job on plaster, sheet rock, or paneling.

Wall-hung cabinets, even if not heavy in themselves, should be fastened to bear the added weight of their contents. Wherever possible, secure them to the studs with lag bolts from two to three inches long.

PART THREE

UNCOMMON SOLUTIONS TO COMMON PROBLEMS

PART THREE

UNCOMMON SOLUTIONS
TO COMMON PROBLEMS

Once you're aware of the difference wall accessories make, you'll want to reappraise your wall treatments. No doubt there are several places where adding a few accessories or rearranging what you now have would create a new excitement without calling for any drastic changes.

There are hundreds of ways to decorate a particular wall. Almost everyone wants to know how to decorate the area surrounding sofas, tables, cabinets, headboards, and pianos, what to do with foyer and hall space, and how to treat wall areas adjacent to windows.

Each illustration in this chapter shows a common problem and suggests an uncommon, exciting way of dealing with it. Whatever your current wall-decorating problem is you will undoubtedly find its counterpart here.

LIVING ROOMS

Clean-lined and simple, the contemporary furniture in this setting is the perfect background for your personal accessory selection. For that important wall area over the sofa, a contemporary mirror is teamed with two Early-American planters to show the effectiveness of using a provincial touch coupled with contemporary design. Refill the planters with fresh flowers to greet each new season.

Fig. 18.

Contemporary living-room furniture, with its geometrically precise lines and angles, contrasts with the cheerful, rambling-branch plaques. The branch plaque chosen is finished in walnut and orange and will always be a friendly note over the wide sofa.

Fig. 19.

Rooms, like people, are sometimes less than perfect in size and proportions. Fortunately, there are decorating tricks you can employ with wall accessories to make the eye see a balanced picture. Below, a large mirror, placed over a table, increases the width of a too-narrow room. The sconces flanking it, the paintings over the easy chair, and the easel picture on the end table also serve a purpose. If the mirror was used alone, the wall would look split in half. Now, however, the eye moves easily and naturally.

Fig. 20.

A stucco fireplace wall with wood trim is the attractive focal point in this thoroughly modern living room. To accessorize the wall in an impressive manner that suits its dramatic simplicity, birds in flight are grouped above the fireplace next to a long, slender planter. To the left is an abstract oil painting.

Fig. 21.

Set in a niche between tall bookcases, a piano requires accessories that give height and are fairly impressive in scale. Here, a painting of a Spanish landscape used with a pair of three-arm sconces furthers the Mediterranean feeling. If a mirror were placed above the piano, it would be distracting to the player.

Fig. 22.

The horizontal area of wall space between a sofa and bookcase wall needs to be filled with important accessories. A wall clock, combining the strong, weighty look of wrought-iron work, bordered by wood does the trick. Strip lighting directly above focuses attention on the long, narrow paintings. A cordless electric clock eliminates unsightly hanging wires.

Fig. 23.

If you are fortunate to have an architecturally interesting wall, flatter it with choice wall accessories. Here, a fireplace and flanking wall panels are outlined by a simple wood-molded trim. The tall, slender planters fit perfectly into the narrow, vertical panels. Their Spanish, wrought-iron look is enhanced by the choice of a boldly carved picture frame over the fireplace.

Fig. 24.

A country-styled living room is enhanced by bringing the outdoors in. The branch plaques placed over the mantel give movement and flow to the wall. Two different-sized pictures placed on the side complete the balance.

Fig. 25.

A delicate balance is achieved in a contemporary room by
combining a number of different objects in an abstract
arrangement. Notice how the eye moves from the small
painting to the right of the fireplace and then up, across
and down to the flower plaque on the left. Placing the
handsome plaque to the side of the fireplace adds interest
and weight to the sitting area.

Fig. 26.

DENS AND FAMILY ROOMS

Shelves and shelves full of books are attractive accessories that give warmth and livability to any room setting. To make the most of your home library, place volumes on random shelves and intersperse them with paintings, plants, plaques, and other accessories. Particularly exciting here are the flamboyant bullfighter plaque and watercolors placed between shelves.

Fig. 27.

Like a spring garden in full bloom, this plaque of sprightly blossoms is both colorful and properly informal for the sitting area of a cozy, contemporary den. A row of pictures under the plaque is balanced by the pictures on an adjacent wall.

Fig. 28.

The rustic, earthy look of a den with zebra skin over a wood-plank floor demands a special touch in accessories. In keeping with the natural, outdoor feeling is a grape plaque that stretches above the sofa. To balance the plaque, two small rectangular pictures are placed at either end, hung low because they're small in scale.

Fig. 29.

The woman who knows how to please a man provides plenty of light and some rugged accessories for his den-office area. A cornice trimmed with wallpaper border conceals built-in lighting that brightens the entire work area, while the desk lamp assures proper wattage for reading and other close work. Note how the clipper-ship plaque answers the need for an important wall accessory to break the expanse of books.

Fig. 30.

Always inviting is the family room that tells something about the pursuits of its occupants. In this case, the interest of six keys over the sofa and a trio of prints depicting antique keys and locks explains graphically the owners' business. They are completely in harmony with the relaxed mood of the furnishings.

Fig. 31.

In a sitting room where both contemporary and traditional furnishings are used, accessories can be the connecting link. The folding screen has a nailhead trim that hints of the Spanish influence and goes well with the nine-arm, Mediterranean-inspired sconce placed over the sofa.

Fig. 32.

Make the most of the fun-and-games atmosphere of a family playroom by doing something lively and colorful with the walls. In this case, the overscaled important fireplace, perfect for the sitting area, is balanced by the boldly carved, iron-gate plaque on the opposite wall.

Fig. 33.

Often in today's home, the family room is a converted garage, porch, or basement, and may still have rough plaster or masonry walls that go well with large-scale, outdoor-type accessories. This remodeled porch has the traditional American-eagle plaque. The eagle has the hearty, natural feeling that complements the rough-textured walls. Next to the eagle is a framed reproduction of a Revolutionary historical document.

Fig. 34.

An oak and iron clock and a pair of hurricane sconces along with a hearty, robust still life contribute to this exciting room in the Mediterranean mood. The modern chrome and glass table with bright flower bouquet gives a perky look.

Everyone has his own idea about wall decoration; that's what makes accessorizing so exciting. Above, an aficionado of the bull ring translates
a hobby into personalized decorating. Adding to the informal beauty of
this intimate setting are the Syroco accent tables, a welcome change from
the usual large cocktail table.

With a quick change of accessories, the same room takes off on a youthful flight of fancy, this time identified with the younger generation by using the patent yellow birds and matching high-gloss planters. The uninhibited use of color in the contemporary painting further adds to the fresh young look.

The cane-patterned fabric of the sofa inspires yet another design treatment. Here, the simplicity of Mondrian-like geometric shapes is the basis of an exciting new collection of wall accessories. Dramatizing the contemporary design are two traditional touches—the Japanese wall screen and the hexagonal chair-side table. One room —three looks—simply by changing accessories.

With contemporary furniture, accessories from any period can be used to create an eclectic room. The quiet, brown-and-black mood of this sitting area suggests the use of color on the walls. Vertical Four Seasons plaques on verde-colored mountings, water-color sketches outlined by green matting, the various pillows used for a softening effect, and the suspended triple light fixtures all have a fresh, contemporary look. The clock adds a Mediterranean feeling and Oriental accessories enhance a modern cube table, which is covered in snake-skin.

The same setting (opposite) assumes an entirely different personality when several of the wall accessories are changed. A more traditional feeling is developed with the use of gilded mirrors, classic figurines and paintings. The collection of miniature mirrors is a unique hobby display treatment.

An occasional change of accessories or even a simple arrangement of furniture can keep your home constantly exciting. A candlelit chandelier and an eighteenth-century Venetian-inspired lavabo and planter elegantly enhance an intimate little area for dining or card playing.

The same area gets a new outlook when the chandelier is replaced by a gilded sconce paired with matching brackets found in Syroco's Saxony Collection. The table is centered on the wall to complete a beautifully balanced grouping.

To create a quiet corner for study or paper work, place the dining table elsewhere and substitute a curved desk that fits nicely in front of the window. For night light, be sure to include a good desk lamp. Remove the more elaborate wall accessories and replace them with paintings, a wall-hung clock and fresh green plants arranged in graduated planters.

If your bedroom is designed to be more than a sleeping room, then the accessories can help set the mood. Here, an elegant mirror over the vanity, pictures and planters lend excitement to the setting.

Photo: courtesy *Better Homes & Gardens*

There is romance in this room, from the fabulous, sheep's-wool rug to the velvety, downy sofa. A majestic, elaborate nine-arm sconce recalls the Louis XV period, with soft candlelight furthering the romantic illusion.

DINING AND BREAKFAST ROOMS

Dining country style suggests a pleasant clutter of objects on the wall. This is accomplished in the setting shown by an open curio cabinet in French-provincial style and a pair of pictures. Balancing this important grouping is a mirror flanked by sconces on an adjacent wall.

Fig. 35.

In a sunny breakfast room, placing the table in front of
the window and treating both the window and surrounding
wall area as a well-coordinated unit gives decorative importance to a small area. The window itself is simply
dressed with trimmed window shades. To one side, over a
dado of wood paneling, are flying-duck plaques. On the
other side is an Early-American clock which is placed below the shelf of books.

Fig. 36.

In a small breakfast room, window and wall decorating is used to achieve eye appeal without overcrowding. Washable, patterned wallpaper, used on the lower part of the wall, is repeated on the window shades. For a cheerful good morning, a bright chanticleer dominates a wall grouping composed of fruit-and-vegetable paintings in varied shapes, sizes, and colors.

Fig. 37.

Besides their decorative value, wall accessories can play an important role in achieving good balance in the placement of furniture. The dining room shown, although modest in size, contains a seven-foot-high armoire, a long and low buffet, table, and chairs. Adding a chandelier would have overcrowded the space. The same romantic effect is achieved by grouping five candles on the table and placing an impressive, nine-arm sconce over the buffet. The sconce adds visual weight and height, balancing the armoire.

Fig. 38.

BEDROOMS

In this age of king-size bedding, the very size of the bed itself makes the headboard wall the focal point of the room. In keeping with the massive scale of a super-size mattress are a trio of Floral-Mates, prettily framed by softly draped panels on either side. Night tables are accessorized differently; a reading lamp on one is balanced by a trio of pictures, linked by leather straps, on the other.

Fig. 39.

From toddler to teen-ager, any boy would feel at home in a room with straightforward contemporary lines in furniture and a hearty outdoor touch in accessories. There is a hint of early Americana in the captain's chair beside the desk and the clipper ship placed above the headboard to balance the bookshelves.

Fig. 40.

There's no need for any bedroom to look stereotyped. Even if a limited amount of floor space dictates the usual bed-dresser-chest arrangement, you can still achieve freshness. Dispense with the usual mirror over the dresser and select a set of traditional four-seasons floral plaques instead. You can have a mirror on another wall, choosing a gilded French-styled one instead of a mirror that matches your bedroom furniture. For a bed of distinction, add a bedspread and wall-hung fabric panel that creates an illusion of bark.

Fig. 41.

For a serene atmosphere that invites relaxation, use sliding, shoji-screen panels at the windows and the simplest of furniture in the room. For ornament, a flock of flying geese above the bed supplies the necessary movement.

Fig. 42.

Perfect balance is achieved in this formally arranged master bedroom. Rising in the center is a group of Floral-Mates plaques that are positioned by you and draw the eye upward. Matching night tables and lamps give unity to this perfect composition.

Fig. 43.

An air of hospitality adds to the charm of this country-style guest bedroom. Overnight visitors feel pleasantly at home when their surroundings are prettied up with plants and pictures. A space-saver as well as an attractive floor plan is the use of a single table between twin beds. The large, provincial planter, hung low over the table, suggests all sorts of colorful arrangements with leaves and dried flowers.

Fig. 44.

KITCHENS AND BATHROOMS

A lot of time is spent in the kitchen. What better reason could there be for using attractive wall accessories? Here, a cordless clock, teamed with the long sweep of a Viking-boat plaque, is hung on the reverse side of kitchen cabinets. This usually neglected wall area brightens each breakfast day.

Fig. 45.

Along with the usual bath accessories that provide comfort
and convenience, include some framed pictures for purely
decorative purposes. In this corner bathroom, paintings are
interspersed with the towel bar, the toothbrush holder, and
the glass shelf. Enclose pictures in glass to prevent steam
damage.

Fig. 46.

A luxurious atmosphere, along with all the comforts, is established in this bath through careful accessorizing. Centered between the double-sink arrangement, a wall-hung floral-decorated soap dish is similarly styled to the twin oval mirrors and towel rings.

Fig. 47.

PART FOUR

WHERE TO
FIND GOOD ACCESSORIES

PART FOUR

WHERE TO
FIND GOOD ACCESSORIES

Individuality in today's interiors can come from accessories rather than furniture. Like the silk-print scarf you add to a basic dress, accessories are the expression of your fashion flair.

For greater variety and interest, you should gather your own personal store of household treasures from more than one period. By keeping a theme in mind, you can be sure the objects you bring together will harmonize with one another.

HEAD FOR THE SHOPPING CENTER

The logical place to start is at the local shopping center. Gift shops, department stores, and furniture stores are particularly helpful when you are considering a large wall area that requires a well-coordinated grouping, for they carry correlated collections of accessories.

These are the best places to find the picture frames, plaques, mirrors, clocks, sconces, or planters that will blend with your room setting. Choose these accessory items with great care, for they can serve as the nucleus of your wall groupings for many years to come.

Visit the model-room sections of your local stores and do some extensive browsing. Take particular notice of what the professional staff designers do with the walls. A clock or mirror you previously saw in the accessory department may strike you as perfect when you see it used in a model interior. All sorts of possibilities will come to mind as you look around. Thus stimulated, you are ready to shop for accessories in the proper frame of mind, determined to give your imagination a treat and actually visualize each object as it would look in a room setting rather than in isolation.

Many stores have fine interior-design services. They can be helpful either to solve a special problem related to choosing accessories or to take over an entire decorating project for you. Services vary greatly in size and scope among individual stores, so make inquiries to find out what is available.

The nice part about using a trained designer is that you have the advantage of his aesthetic knowledge: he will guide you in creating the best environment fitting your personality. A professional designer can save you money by purchasing the right objects. He can also suggest imaginative ways of grouping accessories to give your home distinction.

FINDING ACCESSORIES THAT MIX WITH PERIOD STYLES

You should be looking for the right accessories to blend with the style of a particular interior. Many unique accessories are compatible with the most popular decorating styles, such as:

Early-American. The rustic, hardy appeal of Early-American suggests informal accessories made from pine, nutmeg, oak, or finishes simulating these woods. Also appropriate are objects with the look of copper or some of the simpler hammered, wrought-iron pieces. Plaques or clocks with the traditionally popular inn-keeper-sign shape are always favorites, as are minute-men rifles, costumed pioneer men and women, and game-bird plaques. Most objects that go well with Early-American decor have a flat rather than a shiny look.

American federal and eighteenth-century English. If your home has the more formal flavor of the more prosperous colonial period, avoid rustic accessories. Suitable are mirrors with eagles centered at the top, picture frames with gold finishes, porcelain, glass, and the more delicate Paul Revere silver. The shinier or softly glowing finishes are excellent choices in today's metals.

French and other provincial styles. The provincial furniture of France and neighboring European countries is usually neither as rustic as Early-American nor as formal as eighteenth-century English. Look for accessories that suit an informal yet sophisticated way of life, such as basket carvings and weathervanes, tree plaques, mirrors with floral carvings and latticework designs, pewter, and china. Dried flowers relate particularly well.

Mediterranean. Many different types of accessories fit with the romantic, substantial look of furniture adapted from northern Italian, seventeenth-century, and Spanish styling. Oak and iron objects that are bold,

daring, and overscaled add to the charm of the Mediterranean mood. Since Mediterranean is a flexible style
that allows much latitude, be imaginative. Your choices
will probably be right if you stay away from anything
too delicate in scale.

After acquiring the basic accessories every home
should have, such as mirrors and pictures, you can look
in unexpected places for those extra touches that complete a room and give it character.

TIPS FOR TRAVELERS

Foreign travel can provide one of the most intriguing
markets for marvelous, unusual accessories, provided
you look in the right places.

Avoiding the obvious is the key to enriching your
home with the culture of many lands rather than end-
ing up with items from the souvenir shops. Authentic
accessories that are truly typical of the place you are
visiting lie waiting to be discovered by the adventurous, imaginative tourist.

Ideally, you should study the culture of the country
you're visiting to learn what their special arts and crafts
contributions are. Don't be carried away by "local
color" when you shop in exotic places; remember, the
rules of good decorating still apply. Keep a picture
of your own home in mind and buy what will enhance
your setting.

Among the best sources for acquiring better-quality
travel souvenirs are the antique dealers, flea markets,
and other places patronized by local citizens. There are
still good buys available that mix well with whatever
period you seek. Checking the local paper for events
will supply you with information to current charity
bazaars and fairs.

If you're looking for original paintings or sculpture, you may be delighted at the work done by unknown artists found in summer-resort art colonies. Shopping this way can be a pleasant afternoon diversion.

THE GREAT OUTDOORS

Too often overlooked in the hunt for accessories is the natural beauty that surrounds us, and it is usually yours for the taking.

Seashells, driftwood, wildflowers, autumn leaves, rocks, and pebbles fit into most decorating schemes. They have the unspoiled beauty of nature and can be that extra bit of charm to enhance your collection of man-made accessories.

PLAN FOR ALL SEASONS

Even the best decorating schemes can be varied now and then. A wonderful way to keep your interiors continually fresh is to plan for seasonal changes keyed to whatever is available in your own locale. During the Christmas season, for example, you can gather evergreen branches or holly to supplement the potted plants and fresh flowers.

At winter's end, it's refreshing to introduce a burst of spring-garden colors. Think of dramatic ways to display field flowers, such as in a straw basket. If you own a set of wall-hung planters, have arrangements of dried flowers made up for different seasons of the year and keep rotating them.

In summertime, pack away some of your accessories for a cool, uncluttered look and introduce shells, pebbles, and fresh-cut flowers. If you have a large entrance hall or corner of the living room not in the flow of traffic, use a tall potted palm. Continue the house changing by gathering up all paintings of winter landscapes and substitute sea or mountain scenes.

For autumn, you can reap a rich harvest of decorative beauty by purchasing pumpkins, gourds, or Indian corn, and arranging them in planters or bowls. Baskets of autumn leaves gathered outdoors are pretty and easy on the budget.

Think in terms of interior design when you shop for produce. Later at home, try your hand at arranging the products of nature. You will find yourself developing a new sensitivity to color, form, and texture that will make all future decorating efforts more creative and professional.

MAKING USE OF PLANTS

If you have a choice between using real or artificial plants at home, your decision should always be the live one. There are circumstances, however, when using real plants is impractical and good-quality fool-the-eye artificial plants are available.

Most live plants will live indefinitely with proper watering, cleaning, normal house temperatures, and good light (artificial light is satisfactory).

What plants will go best with your decor? The choice is up to you, for with few exceptions, the natural beauty of greenery fits in everywhere, so choose the leaf and plant formation you happen to like best. Among the hardy, popular choices are these ten:

1. Schefflera. A full, wide-leaf plant growing to five and one-half feet tall and five feet wide. Needs space and direct light.

2. Begonia. A favorite of many, begonias can be grouped together for added effect.

3. Philodendron. Hardy, wide-leaf, strong-branched.

4. Dieffenbachia. Various species of dieffenbachia plants are available and are usually about three to four feet high.

5. Ficus exotica. A small-leafed, tub tree with leaves grouped together at the end of the branch.

6. Kentia palm. Very hardy, Kentia palms fit well with everything and come tall and slim or tall and full. With minor care Kentia palms keep for years, shedding old branches and growing new ones.

7. Dracaena. Similar to the dieffenbachia, ficus, and perennial philodendron, there are many different species of dracaena, and it's a plant that doesn't need much moisture. They can be purchased up to seven feet tall.

8. Small low plants. Among these are the aechmea, African violets, gloxinias, and aeschynanthus. All look well as hanging potted plants. All need ample moisture and good light.

9. Cissus. Also known as grape. Big- or small-leaved, depending on species, they tend to sprawl and can be trained to climb. Artificial (filtered) or weak light will be satisfactory.

10. Boston fern. Also known as nephrolepis. One of the nicest varieties is the Whitmannii, usually found as a tabletop, eighteen-inch-high, potted plant. It needs ample moisture and artificial light.

All the above plants require a minimum of care. They must be properly watered and cleaned: saturation once a week is better than a daily cup of water, and bathing once every six weeks in a bathtub will keep the leaves green and enable them to breathe.

HOW TO USE HOBBY COLLECTIONS

With so much emphasis placed by designers on getting a personal touch into your interiors, displaying hobby collections ranks high on the list. Nothing is more delightful than a room that tells something about its occupants at first glance. It's a fine idea to display accessories that reveal your personality and interests. Displaying a theme that absorbs the entire family, such as sailing, bird-watching, or photography, is a good way to personalize your room. Place a hobby collection in surroundings that are best suited to it, such as recreation rooms, studios, or dens.

In provincial rooms, collections of old china, pottery, pewter, glass, coins, maps, costumed dolls, and similar objects have a great deal of charm. To avoid a helter-skelter, cluttered look, keep them grouped together. Coin collections look best when framed and hung in groups. The same display techniques can be used with stamps, butterflies, historic documents, and other flat objects, such as family photographs.

MAKING YOUR OWN ACCESSORIES

Using handmade items of your own artwork can add immeasurably to the personality of your home. Your own hooked rugs, ceramics, woven baskets, embroidery, tapestry, crewelwork, sketches, and paintings should be displayed.

For those who enjoy the satisfaction of doing handicrafts, yet haven't the talent to start from scratch, some of the finish-it-yourself kits now on the market offer a chance to acquire professional designs. A simple and satisfying creative project can now be found in a new series of wall plaques that you can paint and glaze yourself. All the paints and materials needed are included in the kit, along with suggestions on which colors to use. You can, though, paint the plaque to suit your own color preference. Subjects of available plaques vary from birds and flowers to sailing ships, old keys, sconces, and scenes of primitive Americana.

HOW TO BUDGET YOUR ACCESSORIES DOLLARS

Once you know where to find the right accessories, the big decision is how to allocate your budget.

Since accessories, despite their importance, are usually the last items to be put into place, most people are tempted to compensate by spending less than originally planned on the finishing touches. This is similar to buying an expensive dress and wearing it with cheap jewelry, shoes, and handbag. If you've run out of sufficient funds, it's wiser to be patient, acquiring one good accessory at a time.

Splurging on one great accessory now and adding companion pieces later is a sensible idea. As a matter of fact, the room that takes shape gradually often emerges as the most beautiful, since each item is carefully considered and chosen with unruffled calm.

If your goal is to acquire an ensemble of wall accessories in a particular style, finish, or period, it's important that you make the initial selection from a line that is well known, reliable, and readily available at stores of good reputation. Don't make the mistake of starting off with an irresistible "bargain" from a line that has been discontinued; you may never be able to find anything to match. When buying basic accessories, such as clocks, mirrors, and picture frames, buy the best quality you can afford. Cheap mirrors soon become cloudy or distorted, clocks that don't keep time are a nuisance, and frames that discolor or warp are all worthless acquisitions.

If you can't afford the original oil paintings you hope to own, choose good reproductions, prints, and watercolors. Use of poster art is an inexpensive method of filling in the bare spots.

It makes a great deal of sense for young married couples, military couples, and others who occupy temporary quarters to economize on furniture and concentrate on buying good accessories. Good mirrors, clocks, sconces, and pictures are easily portable and arrangeable against new walls. So if you're just starting to furnish a home and don't expect to remain, buy only the essentials of furniture and cover the walls with colorful wall-accessory arrangements.

PART FIVE

THE WORLD OF COLOR

PART FIVE

THE WORLD OF COLOR

If accessories are the cosmetics applied to a room, then color can be likened to the sparkle in a woman's eye.

Deciding on a color scheme is the fun part of decorating, for color is lively, stimulating, and constantly exciting to the emotions. Since color is everywhere, from the four walls to the smallest accessory, nothing in the room is more important than the right color combination. Be mindful that it costs no more to use rich, clean colors than it does to use tired, dull ones. By knowing how to get the most out of color, you can impart decorative richness to a room completed on a modest budget.

THE ROLE OF ACCESSORIES

To keep your interiors from becoming bland, you should use color to freshen a room without going to any great expense. This can be done by basing your color scheme on a neutral background that will serve as a foil for any brilliantly colored accents used within the room. Any room can be transformed simply by changing colored accessories while leaving the basics as they are. Switch throw pillows used on the sofa, change picture mattings used, change colored candles used in candlesticks—all these will transform a room.

THE PSYCHOLOGY OF COLOR

Color, like weather, brings about swings of mood that range from exhilaration to depression. Just as we react favorably to a bright, sunny day and share in the gloom of an unfriendly, overcast day, we also get a psychological lift from entering a colorful, cheery room. We likewise feel depressed when our surroundings are gray or overly dull.

Trends in colors are influenced by world events. The solemnity of World War II resulted in drab khaki color schemes, followed by a postwar rebellion against austerity that brought bright blue, chartreuse, and red-orange to the fore.

The colors you choose say a lot about your outlook and personality. Cheerful, outgoing persons lean toward the warm color families of yellow, red, and orange, while the more reserved person is likely to prefer the cool blues and greens.

The correct color choice can minimize architectural defects, make small rooms look larger, and bring cheer into dark, sunless interiors. Color is among the most valuable tools available in decorating.

WHERE TO FIND INSPIRATION

Narrowing your choice is a difficult challenge that

can be made easier if you have a simple planning guide. Almost any familiar object, large or small, can lead you to choosing a good color scheme. The combination you are seeking may be taken from any of these sources:

1. A pattern that pleases you. While shopping, you may see a bolt of fabric, a wallpaper sample, or a patterned area rug that stirs your imagination. Chances are a closer examination will reveal the two main colors, with one accent color, in this pattern that could provide you with a ready-made scheme. Suppose you find a print with daffodil-yellow flowers, green leaves, and an egg-white background. Paint the walls the egg-white, use the print for curtains, and quilt it for a bedspread, select a daffodil-yellow rug fringed with white cotton, and use the green as an accent color in lamp shades. For seasonal changes, use a bowl of fresh yellow daffodils and change the pictures to twin wall plaques.

2. An important painting. Some of the loveliest, most harmonious color schemes begin with inspiration from a painting. When the two major colors in the painting are repeated in furniture and accessories, the result will be a pleasing balance. Multicolored wall accessories, for instance a plaque depicting a basket of flowers, can serve the same purpose.

3. Check your wardrobe. The homemaker who is timid about color within her home may be a whiz at planning the right color accents for her dress. For example, if you have a flair for choosing colorful scarves, there is no reason why this color sense can't be carried over into your home furnishings.

4. Be aware of nature. Bringing the outdoors in is a way of creating exciting schemes, for there is no more adept master of color than nature. Decide what you admire most about the natural world outside your window. If it's New England's fall foliage, a color scheme of russet, brown, and green may be correct for you. If you prefer spring flowers, study a still-life Van Gogh print for color relationships. If your happiest moments have been gazing at trees against the blue sky, you would no doubt be at home in a blue-green interior.

5. *Study model-room settings or photographs of interiors*. Using a model room as a guide is a good way, but bring in some innovations of your own. Remember that model rooms are designed for visual effect. Because the room is done by a professional, the advantage of finding a model room or a color photograph that suits you is that it shows how much of each color to use and in what proportions.

6. *Consult an interior designer*. Since color is so important and can do so much for your home, it might be wise to invest in consultation with an expert. After discussions with you and your husband, he can help you decide which colors are best, and which colors you should avoid.

FAD OR FASHION

Color fashions in home furnishings change with the times, and you shouldn't follow the fads just for change.

If you are, however, sold on such a new scheme and it is composed of colors you like best, chances are you won't tire of it. Recent examples of color schemes that have what it takes to last, despite the fact that they came into being as "the latest vogue" are red, white, and blue; also fern-apple green, usually mixed with shocking pink.

Put more color and interest on the walls to brighten your bedroom. From Syroco's collection of Floral-Mates, the carved plaques flank a headboard made exciting with a few yards of bedspread fabric.

Pick a pretty drapery pattern and take your color scheme from it—neutral walls, blue and brown repeated in the rug, just enough orange in the chair fabric, and some wood-finished wall accessories in medium brown tones. The Syroco mirror, sconces, shelf and clock are correlated to make decorating easier.

Opposite: Related color schemes made up of two cool colors are restful and easy on the eyes. For contrast, inserts of wood paneling are used within strong blue frameworks. Accessories are arranged in curio cabinets and on shelves flanking the curved fireplace. The planter, exuberantly filled with dried flowers, adds a softening touch to the wall.

All eyes are on the wall arrangement in a dining area that comes alive with vibrant color. A varied accessories collection is "framed" by wood trim and dramatized by the rich, deep yellow background color. Contrasting with the soft look of old map prints and mellow wood plaques are Syroco's bright multicolored fruit basket, plants and pewter objects. Colors are inspired by paisley wallpaper used below the counter and as matching table cover fabric.

To the young in heart, color is all the more exciting when its tempo is stepped up by slick and shiny finishes. Keyed to the lacquered look in decorating are sprightly, stylized plaques that give fresh new faces to fish, birds and fowl. For added good measure, there's a table skirted in vinyl with a patent-leather gleam.

Inspired by a wallpaper pattern (opposite), you can venture into such unique color schemes as green, golden-yellow and orange. Set it off with a set of color-coordinated bathroom accessories. The group shown, including mirror, towel rings, shelves and other necessities, is in fashionable moss green. The step stool slides under the sink when not in use.

For the scheme that never lets you down, start with neutral backgrounds and then introduce printed fabrics in the colors you love. The room is enhanced by Syroco's thirteenth-century wrought iron sconce reproduction and the warmth of leather-bound books. Only the upholstered pieces need be slipcovered to give a new color scheme.

The patina of old gold, as well as similar design motifs, coordinates the fern-filled planters with the oval mirror. The sofa print mixes well with the thin-striped wall and drapery fabric in this formal living room.

A room with a bold, contrasting color scheme—orange, green and yellow —takes on added depth from the elegance of a single important accessory grouping. Deep-carved, free-flowing wood-branch plaques centered over the fireplace add richness and character to the wall.

With a definite color scheme and careful accessory touches, a hallway can contribute to the decorative appearance of your home. The large mirror and correlated Mediterranean accessories, combined with the two rush chairs, give a room-size look to what is really a small area.

CHOOSING COLORFUL ACCESSORIES

If you've never before looked upon wall accessories as an integral part of a color scheme, try a different approach with your next interior and see what you've been missing.

As the largest single expanse of space for decorating, walls must make an important color contribution or the total effect of your color scheme will not meet the requirements of good balance and proportion. While it is usually best to limit the number of colors selected for a room to two, with one additional as an accent, color itself is meant to be used all over. Improper color distribution has the same uneven look that results when you place all the heavy pieces of furniture together.

Inseparable to a designer are the relationships between color and pattern. If some people tend to fear color, many more are so much afraid of pattern that they avoid it completely. The surest way of introducing pattern safely is to use wall accessories and other smaller items as your major pattern source.

Dark-painted or wallpapered walls may require a little more discretion in handling accessories, but the dramatic effects possible are well worth any extra effort. Use light, contrasting colored objects on dark walls, and choose simple, square picture frames to delineate the paper pattern with the picture.

If you have an already completed interior that lacks color and pattern, adding wall accessories may be all that is necessary.

Collections of decorative objects offer another source of pattern and color to perk up a bland room. A set of decorative china dishes displayed on a plate rack will relieve the starkness of a plain wall. Also helpful are framed butterflies, coins against felt backgrounds, and small curio cabinets holding colored glass.

PROPORTION

A good scheme demands more than simply choosing colors that go together. It is equally important to use the right amount of each color. One color should always predominate, meaning it should account for approximately two-thirds of the room's surfaces. When two colors share the spotlight, the end result is bound to be unsatisfactory, for seeing equally large areas of two different colors upsets a room's balance. Next, a secondary color should be used in smaller amounts. Finally, a third color should be chosen for accent.

To make this formula work for you, gather samples of the fabrics, floor, and wall coverings you plan to use. Cut them to the correct proportionate sizes and place them out on the room's floor plan. Don't forget to include wall and ceiling colors—these five sides represent the largest color areas. Color them in with crayons to get the right effect.

Following this procedure will enable you to arrive correctly at color balance.

TYPES OF COLOR SCHEMES

Getting too technical about color may spoil the fun, so don't burden yourself with precise technical terminology, but it is helpful to know the standard three-color-scheme variations.

Monochromatic. The one-color scheme is made up of several tints and shades of the same color and usually includes some white or black. It has a relaxing effect that makes it especially suitable for formal living rooms and master bedrooms.

Analogous or related. The second type of scheme makes use of two or three colors from the same half of the color wheel, such as blue and green, lying adjacent on one side, or yellow-red-orange, chosen from the colors on the opposite side of the wheel.

Complementary or contrasting. The third type of scheme begins with two colors directly opposite each other—one warm, the other cool. Yellow with blue, or green with red are examples of contrasting schemes.

WOOD CONTRIBUTES COLOR

Not to be overlooked in planning a color scheme is the wood furniture in a room, for wood has color and is usually present in fairly substantial amounts. While wood finishes throughout a room need not match exactly, they should blend rather than contrast for a harmonious whole.

Since deep browns are warm and intense, they will give an entirely different effect than the light-to-medium wood tones. Painted-furniture finishes will also contribute to the overall color scheme. Generally speaking, light woods look well against the contrast of darker backgrounds, and vice versa. Painted finishes look well against pastel walls.

HOW LIGHTING AFFECTS COLOR

Lighting, whether natural or artificial, dictates the final effect of your color scheme. Pale colors and shiny finishes reflect light, making the area appear brighter, while light is absorbed by dark colors and dull finishes. You should, therefore, consider the daylight exposure of a room before deciding on a color scheme. Rooms that get a great deal of sunlight may have to be darkened with cool colors, while the reverse holds for rooms that are shaded for the better part of the day. At night, be sure to increase the wattage planned if your color scheme is dark, as deep-toned colors absorb light.

CREATING ILLUSIONS

Few rooms are perfect in size, proportions, or architectural details. But with color as an ally, you can fool the eye and correct bad proportions or poor details.

1. The long and narrow shape. The principle that dark colors come forward and light colors recede may be used to change the room's shape. If a room is long in relation to its width, make the end walls advance by painting them darker shades. The same principle will elongate a square. Patterned wallpaper could also bring that section forward.

2. The too high ceiling. An area usually overlooked in decorating, the ceiling can be either emphasized or made inconspicuous with color. The low-ceilinged room requires a lighter paint color than the walls to make it seem higher. A high ceiling can be lowered by painting it darker or by decorating it with patterned wallpaper.

3. The small room with a closed-in feeling. Using light colors for the walls, floor, and ceiling will push back all the surfaces and give a more open feeling to the diminutive room. Follow through by using light curtain fabrics that blend in with the surrounding walls, and slipcovering bulky, upholstered pieces in similar pastel colors.

4. The open floor plan found in small houses or apartments. Although necessary and desirable for creating an illusion of spaciousness in modern housing, the open floor plan requires a special color plan. If color schemes clash between one area and the next, the effect will be jarring; if they are too similar, they will be monotonous. For a balanced effect, use the same colors in reverse proportions in different areas, such as a predominately blue living room with green accents leading into a predominately green dining area with blue accents.

Most importantly use color as an ally. Don't fear it —color is part of our daily lives and a happy part at that!

GLOSSARY OF COLOR TERMS

The Primary Colors: Yellow, red, and blue. All colors derive from these.

·*The Secondary Colors:* Green (yellow and blue), orange (red and yellow), and mauve (red and blue).

The Tertiary Colors: Any color that lies between the primary and secondary colors, such as red-purple, blue-green, yellow-orange, or vice versa.

The Neutral Colors: Black, white, and pure gray.

Color Intensity: The degree of purity of pigment in a color; brightness.

Hue: The name of a color.

Tint: The lightness in a color. By adding white, red becomes pink. More white will make it a baby pink.

Shade: The opposite of tint. By adding black to a color, a darker hue is developed.

The Warm Colors: Reds, oranges, and yellows.

The Cool Colors: Blues, greens, and mauves.

PART SIX

SHEDDING LIGHT
ON WALL ART

PART SIX

SHEDDING LIGHT
ON WALL ART

You'll be amazed to see what good lighting can do to dramatize wall accessories. Properly illuminated, with neither glare nor gloom to detract, a room assumes a special glow that will impart an extra measure of warmth and charm.

To plan a lighting scheme, start by making a list of the room's activities—dining, reading, games, conversation, television viewing. Various activities require different illumination.

Studies and home offices. The desk area demands illumination that covers the entire surface without shadows or glare. Be sure the center of the lamp shade is at eye level for the seated person. Glare will result if the eye is above or below the shade. For best light, choose an opaque shade with a white inner lining.

Dining. Since different moods are desired in a dining area, candelabra bulbs on a dimmer switch are ideal. Start out bright, if you wish, then dim the fixture to create a mellow, friendly atmosphere for dessert-and-coffee time. Candles on the table are also helpful in creating atmosphere; however, keep them tall, with the flame above a person's eye level.

Living room. Most living rooms require at least five lighting sources to bring about the proper light balance. One simple way of judging whether or not light is correctly diffused is to remember that each lamp can illuminate an area of about thirty-five to forty-five square feet. Compute the number of lighting fixtures needed. The typical living room requires three levels of intensity: dimness for music appreciation, medium light for television watching, and bright light for conversation. Dim lighting has the psychological effect of making guests less enthusiastic for lively discussion. For an easy way to achieve this low-medium-high light change, use dimmers and three-way-bulb lamps. Try using different types of lighting to avoid monotony: table lamps, floor lamps, valance lighting, wall brackets, and floor canisters. For bookshelves and wall-hung cabinets, install shelf-strip lighting that illuminates both up and down.

Kitchen. Start with an overhead light, which is usually fluorescent, and supplement it with strip lighting placed above the work counters. Often you'll use this under-the-cabinets lighting without the overhead.

Family room. The most lived-in room in the house should be evenly well lighted to provide for the many activities that will take place and to maintain the bright atmosphere desired. Avoid sharp contrasts of light in this all-purpose room. Determine the number of square feet, as you did for the living room, and provide enough lamps and other fixtures to cover the area. You should include a chandelier or high hats (recessed or surface-mounted ceiling fixtures) over a card table. The use of shelf lighting or recessed ceiling fixtures in front of bookcases is helpful in giving correct illumination.

Bedrooms. Today, bedrooms that double as sitting rooms, studies, or sewing rooms are great assets. To do this, you must give special attention to lighting requirements. A chandelier with a dimmer is excellent for providing a pre-bedtime, relaxed atmosphere. For grooming, use twin wall brackets, face-height, flanking a mirror. A light inside the closet, preferably with an automatically operated on-off switch, is also a great convenience. In order that one person may read while another sleeps, use a high-intensity lamp on the night table or attached to the headboard for the reader.

SPECIAL EFFECTS FOR WALL ACCESSORIES

If the overall lighting scheme is good, your accessories will benefit wherever they're placed.

For important paintings, use clip-on light units that attach to the picture frame and cast shadow-free light.

A gallery-effect grouping of several paintings or a montage of pictures combined with three-dimensional accessories may be accented uniquely with wall-washers, surface-mounted or recessed. You can use any number required and space them as needed.

For the most decoratively impressive wall in the room, cornice lighting gives even illumination and accent to the furniture and accessories below. (Fig. 48.)

In a kitchen, the wall space between counter and cabinets is a good place for pictures or plaques. Use

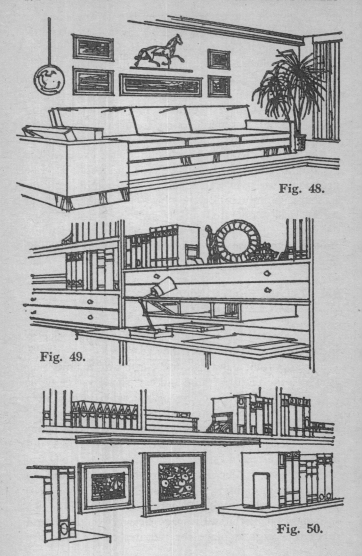

Fig. 48.

Fig. 49.

Fig. 50.

strip lighting under the counters to brighten your decorator touches.

If you want to light a wall and can't ceiling-recess the fixtures, place the wall-washer type of canister on top of a cabinet, having it reflect up and onto your wall accessories.

Pole lamps are handy. You can adjust the individual lamps to spotlight your wall, then redirect them when needed for reading or other close work.

A new, versatile spotlight is the high-intensity lamp. Placed on a desk, it can be directed at a framed photograph when not in use for paperwork. High-intensity lamps are also effective when set on shelves to spotlight individual pieces. (Fig. 49.)

Wall-hung furniture, from the smallest curio cabinet to the complete wall-to-wall, floor-to-ceiling unit, benefits from special lighting, such as strip lights attached to bookshelves. (Fig. 50.) Objects inside a wall niche can be lit by using glass shelves and placing a fluorescent lamp at the top covered with a sandblasted glass ceiling. For larger expanses of built-in shelving and furniture, use ceiling-mounted fixtures placed fifteen inches in front of the unit for even light distribution.

If you're using live plants in wall-hung containers, flank them with wall-bracket lighting. This will not only add to the decorative value of the arrangement but also nurture a plant that possibly receives insufficient natural light.

PART SEVEN

POPULAR STYLES IN
FURNITURE AND ACCESSORIES

PART SEVEN

POPULAR STYLES IN FURNITURE AND ACCESSORIES

Which home-furnishings style is best for you and your family?

There is far more available than ever before for the interior of your home. Thanks to today's mass-production methods and techniques, manufacturers can now duplicate the handcrafted designs of past centuries and offer them at reasonable consumer prices.

Gathering together designs from many different periods to complete a room is a twentieth-century innovation. With the world growing smaller, we are all made aware of the rich variety of styles available. Rather than making just one style choice, we combine two or more periods in the same house, or even in the same room. There is a glorious new decorating freedom available to plan your own home around the things you like and enjoy.

Provided the planning is done within the bounds of good taste, this is a good development. It can help to make your home individual, even though the same apartment or house layout is found multiplied throughout the country.

HOW TO BLEND DECORATING STYLES

Mixing, rather than matching, referred to by professionals as "eclectic" decorating, is here to stay. The combining possibilities are endless. To show how flexible interior design has become, all of the following mixtures can be used today:

1. Contemporary furniture mixed with traditional accessories and accent pieces.

2. Contemporary mixed with provincial furniture and provincial country accessories.

3. Traditional case goods mixed with contemporary upholstery. Here contemporary accessories and sculpture can be used effectively.

4. Simple, Oriental-styled room backgrounds combined with European eighteenth-century designs.

Don't be frightened by eclectic decorating. By following the usual rules of form and good taste you can easily learn how to mix and match. Keep to a similar feeling in choosing items and you'll be on the correct path.

Notice the motifs on furniture and accessories. The designs of two separate historical periods or of two different countries often utilize the same decorative details. This can be a clue to you that they will blend and mix together. Eighteenth-century French and Italian periods, for example, make use of lavish flowing romantic ornamental details—ribbons, garlands, and gilding. Joining two curved Louis XV armchairs with a simple, straight-line, lacquered and chrome cabinet within the same room can achieve a sleekness and sophistication of design. With this scheme add an eighteenth-century-inspired Italian mirror.

Look for connecting links. You can combine different elements when they have something in common, such as a repetition of the same colors used in both plain and patterned upholstery fabric. You can also combine furniture of different periods by using the same upholstery fabrics on the various pieces.

Learn by professional example. Good examples of mix-and-match design abound. They're found in movie settings, home-furnishings books, shelter magazines, and the room displays featured in furniture and department stores. If you see a combination you like, use it as a guide when planning a room. Eventually observing the work of others will teach you to recognize signs of compatibility. Remember, good taste encompasses more than one style or period.

Consult a designer. Professional designers are able to bring together correctly what would, at first glance, appear the most unlikely elements. With your own ideas of how you wish to live combined with the designer's knowledge of what should be done, the results can be refreshing.

Plan ahead. If you are enthusiastic about combining different styles, it is doubly important to have a complete plan formulated before you make your first purchase. Although accessories and other decorative details are usually purchased last, you should be thinking about them when you commence planning a room. Keeping the total picture in mind as you make each purchase is the secret of successful coordination.

ACCESSORIZING IN THE
TRADITIONAL STYLES

If you're strictly a traditionalist and prefer living with one or two similar periods, you no doubt have a clear idea of the finished effect you desire. Follow through with accessories and make selections easily from the varied merchandise available in the style of your choice. Do include some personalized accessories, however, so your room will have character and a lived-in look.

Even though your favorite pieces of pottery, picture frames, and other family heirlooms are not of the same period, you will find they can group together. A traditional hutch, curio cabinet, or bookcase can be used as a display case for diverse accessories.

For the well-coordinated look, one strategically placed wall grouping composed of a few important objects such as a traditional mirror and pair of sconces placed over a mantel is more effective than a profusion of smaller objects.

While the lines of most traditional furniture suggest formal balance, this by no means rules out the more adventurous placement. You can and should experiment.

ACCESSORIZING PROVINCIAL SETTINGS

Warm, homelike, and charming, the provincial furniture styles lend themselves to an informal kind of accessorizing.

The more rustic types of provincial, such as Early-American and Country-French, suggest a pleasant clutter of objects imaginatively displayed in informal arrangements. In addition to the few specially chosen objects like clocks, plaques, and planters, you can display the everyday household objects that were often the only "accessories" the French farmer or early-American housewife possessed—wooden utensils, copper molds, pewter mugs, and iron trivets on the kitchen walls, or the more decorative china, ironstone, or earthenware objects for living and dining rooms.

More refined provincial furniture calls for somewhat less clutter and more emphasis on having a few important objects chosen to enhance and brighten the overall style of the room.

CONTEMPORARY ACCESSORIZING

Clean-lined, uncluttered, and free of any surface decoration, modern styles allow you a free hand in accessorizing a room. Working against a background of white or light-painted walls with no architectural detail, you should strive to get color, texture, and pattern into your accessories.

Ingenuity, not only in choice of objects but also in their arrangement, makes contemporary room planning exciting. There are no set rules to follow, since modern is of today. More so than any other style, here you can use accessories to achieve a truly creative personalized effect.

It is wise to concentrate on one outstanding wall grouping. It can make a big impact. A large abstract painting in primary colors, an unusual free-form sculpture, a sunburst clock or a lacquered mirror—any of these can be the nucleus around which to build a highly individualized accessory collection. If the effect you want is one of organized clutter, you might devote an entire hallway to an informal arrangement of many objects. Use only one wall, however; don't force the eye to dart both ways.

A GUIDE TO HOME-FURNISHINGS STYLES

Whether you decide to mix or match, a knowledge of the styles that are currently popular is helpful.

Traditional Styles

In traditional furniture and accessories you can recapture some of the romance, nostalgia, and tranquillity of other centuries, when life was more leisurely. Traditional backgrounds need not be stiff, formal, or imposing. Properly executed, they have as much youth, vitality, and freshness as today's colorful creations.

The traditional styles have survived the test of time because they are good, honest designs that are functional and suitable for daily living. In the historical monarchies of Europe, where our present period designs derive from, it was customary for the royal families to establish the style and encourage the arts. That's why most period styles are named for the monarch in whose reign they were created. Thus we have Queen Anne, Louix XV, and others. Today we also refer to an eighteenth-century design by giving the designer's name. Among the great trend-setting English eighteenth-century designers were such names as Thomas Chippendale, Thomas Sheraton, George Hepplewhite, and the Adam brothers.

While genuine antiques of the great home-furnishings periods are rare, good reproductions and adaptations are in abundance at moderate prices. This is particularly true of accessories. Thus a reasonable facsimile of the hand-carved mirror and matching sconces that once hung in the halls of Versailles can now be enjoyed in the foyer of your own home. In many cases, contemporary reproductions of furniture and

Queen Anne

Fig. 51.

accessories are properly scaled in size or interpreted in simple adaptations to make them more suitable for to-day's smaller rooms.

Eighteenth-Century English

The eighteenth century is known as the golden age of the English cabinetmakers. During these fruitful de-sign years England produced some of the finest and most exquisite designs in its entire home-furnishings history. Because our own country is so closely linked with England historically, the great traditional English styles have always been popular in America.

Queen Anne (1702–1714). Queen Anne furniture influenced designers in the American colonies. Still popular, the Queen Anne style suits today's interiors because it is decorative yet simple. Among its out-standing characteristics is the cabriole leg—a graceful curve that often ends in a claw-and-ball foot. Another favorite motif is the scallop-shell ornament found on table aprons, cabinets, and accessories. Highboys were topped by broken or scroll pediments. Tea drinking developed to a fine art at this time, inspiring the oc-casional table designs modern hostesses find so handy for informal serving. The Oriental influence appeared in the use of lacquered finishes, sometimes with painted decoration. Walnut was the favored wood, although mahogany began to predominate before the end of the period.

For wall treatments, wood paneling was widely used as background. Decorative wallpapers began to appear more and more. Selection of decorative acces-sories was still somewhat limited to sconces, pictures, and tapestries, and remained so until the late eigh-

Chippendale

Fig. 52.

teenth century. Mirrors, popular but expensive, came with the glass made in two pieces. Queen Anne mirrors were handsomely framed in veneered woods, and the tops repeated the broken-pediment style of highboys. A new shape developed was the long, narrow mirror with two panels of glass joined in the center. In the Early-Georgian period, which overlapped the Queen Anne period, more ornate, carved, and gilded frames were in favor. The architectural look also became popular in wall mirrors with pilasters at the sides and pediments at the top.

Chippendale (*1727–1779*). Inspired by Queen Anne, Louis XV, and the eighteenth-century English-Oriental travel, Thomas Chippendale created a style of furniture with exquisite proportion and diverse designs. Working in mahogany, he developed the art of wood carving to a perfection that has never been surpassed. As is true with most designers, he is famous for his chairs. Still popular today are the Chinese Chippendale adaptations—bamboo turns on chair and table legs, Chinese fretwork detail on linear bases, lacquer finishes, and the familiar camel-back sofa with straight-legged base.

The mirrors Chippendale created are outstanding, for here his skill at carving unusual shapes and designs is seen most clearly. Gilded frames were the rule, and his choice of ornamental motifs ranged from classic to rococo birds, ribbons, leaves, and intricately curved lines swirling about oval- or rectangular-shaped glass.

Hepplewhite and Sheraton (*1760–1806*). George Hepplewhite's contribution was his emphasis on the achievement of elegance through understatement—slender lines, simple and slightly tapered legs, graceful

Hepplewhite and
Sheraton

Fig. 53.

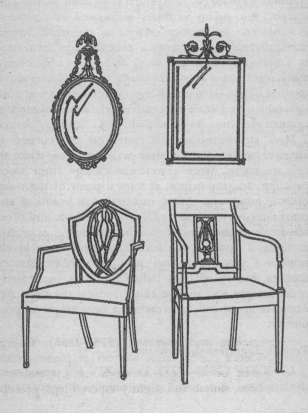

proportions, and a minimum of decoration. He used serpentine curves on sideboards, and is known for his shield-back chairs. His straight-legged chairs had detail centered on the backs.

The restrained influence of Hepplewhite and Sheraton furniture design carried into accessories. Sconces, mirrors, and frames were sprinkled with fluting, ribbons, wheat blossoms, rosettes, and medallions.

Adam (1762–1794). Architects as well as cabinetmakers, the Adam brothers influenced room backgrounds and accessories as well as furniture. In the latter part of the eighteenth century, the excavation at Pompeii created a revival of Greek and Roman classicism. Adam furniture made use of classic architectural details—columnar legs on sideboards and console tables, and such decorative details on cabinets as egg-and-dart moldings, wreaths, and acanthus leaves.

Most significant at this time was the change in interior backgrounds. Plaster walls, painted white or delicate colors, were a welcome change from wood paneling, and the mantel as a focal point of the room became important. Adam mantels were beautiful and ornamented with swags, ribbons, urns, frets, and other classic symbols. Against this background, decorative accessories came to the fore. Designers made lovely urns and vases, porcelain plaques, mirrors, statues, sconces, and chandeliers. Italian paintings, particularly of landscapes and ancient ruins, became the rage. Accessories in general had reached a new height in popularity.

French Traditional Furniture

Louis XIV (1643–1715). Louis XIV is a period with the emphasis on decoration and richness in detail. Much

Adam

Fig. 54.

of the interior detail work popularized the creation of decorative accessories—clocks, sconces, and candelabra. Furniture was massive in scale and built on rectangular lines. Embellishment ranged from carving and gilding to elaborately patterned inlays of wood, ivory, mother-of-pearl, brass, and porcelain.

Accessories were made of gold, crystal, or porcelain. Clocks were introduced, both standing and wall varieties, and they were apt to be elaborately carved and gilded. Among the motifs associated with this period is the classic sunburst—emblem of Louis XIV—still widely used today in the design of clocks and wall mirrors.

Louis XV (1723–1774). Surrounded by beautiful women in his court, Louis XV allowed them to influence the styles. Furniture became smaller in scale and more graceful in line, with gentle curves replacing some of the heavy, rectilinear lines of Louis XIV. Delicate ornamentation was applied with a lavish hand. Noteworthy was the appearance of many new pieces we would refer to today as occasional furniture— charming writing desks, inviting chaise longues, and small tables for serving, card games, or chair-side use. It was a style emphasizing comfort and one that appeals to feminine tastes.

Accessories changed greatly during this period. Feminine and romantic motifs flourished on decorative mirrors, clocks, sconces, and other ornaments—cupids, shepherdesses, lyres, violins, and other musical instruments, cockleshells, and floral motifs. A mirror and candles became standard decoration over mantelpieces. In fabrics, cotton prints arrived to supplement the more sumptuous silks and velvets, and the French toile patterns (pastoral scenes) we still use today were used

Louis XIV

Fig. 55.

Louis XV

Fig. 56.

Louis XVI

Fig. 57.

for the first time. Painting, gilding, and Chinese lacquer were applied to wall accessories.

Louis XVI (1774–1789). The emphasis on luxury that marked the two previous periods continued, but in a more subdued fashion. There was a revival of classic motifs and simplified geometric forms. Occasional furniture and everyday conveniences continued to inspire designers, who turned out drop leaf dining tables, writing tables, and game tables of every description.

Accessories became more abundant and attracted greater interest as an integral part of interior decoration. In many upper-class homes, room backgrounds were being simplified, and painted, papered, or fabric-covered walls were replacing the usual lavish wood paneling. This led to a demand for greater variety in wall accessories: clocks, mirrors, and barometers of gilded bronze, and all types of paintings—oils, watercolors, and simple drawings. Books, statues, and the small lacquered boxes and other ornaments of the Far East were displayed. Even table lamps began to appear as the interest in better lighting grew. The little *bouillotte* lamp that we still use today was designed during this era.

Directoire and Empire (1789–1815). One of the duties of the Directoire, a governing board that ruled France after the Revolution, was to create a new school of interior design. Simplicity replaced excessive luxury, and classic symbols prevailed, with the emphasis on motifs of Italy and Egypt, where Napoleon was currently waging successful wars. Elaborate carving, gilding, and the too-much-of-everything court style gave way to moderation. Furniture was straight-lined for the most part and relieved by a small amount of

Directoire and
Empire

Fig. 58.

detail—brass lion's-paw feet on chairs and tables, lyre backs for mahogany chairs and settees, brass or copper rails outlining occasional tables.

During the reign of Emperor Napoleon that quickly followed, known as the Empire period in furniture design, furniture took on masculine-oriented proportions and gained a solid, substantial look. For the most part, decoration consisted of military symbols and personalized tributes to the Napoleonic victories—eagles, torches, crossed swords, Egyptian sphinxes and caryatids, laurel wreaths surrounding the letter "N," and the traditional Napoleonic bumblebee.

Accessories, too, emphasized the military and classic symbols of Egypt and Rome. Bronze clocks with Egyptian statuettes, busts of Napoleon, and paintings of the Emperor were prevalent. Floor-standing mirrors on swivel bases, decorated with ormolu mounts, were frequently used as accessories and became known as psyches.

American Traditional Styles

Early-American (1617–1720). The first American settlers found little time for gracious living. There were houses to be built, fields to be tilled, and cloth to be spun. Except for a few pieces that some families managed to bring with them from England, furniture had to be made with what simple tools and materials were available. Out of this background of necessity grew a style of furniture that was honest, simple, and very practical. There was little carving or applied ornament, and everything was made with function uppermost in mind. The kitchen, center of family activity, doubled as dining and sitting room. The bed-

Colonial

Fig. 59.

room was simply furnished with a bed and storage chest.

Decorative accessories were scarce. Plate and spoon racks served the dual function of filling in the bare spots on walls and providing additional storage space in sparsely furnished houses. Rifles, candlesticks, fireplace accessories, pictures, and maps breathed life and color into stark interiors. Clocks had to be imported until the eighteenth century and were virtually nonexistent among the early settlers, while mirrors were expensive and also considered in the luxury class. The first clock-making factories appeared around 1700, and made impressive wall and mantel clocks. Later, original American designs were created, the most famous of which is the banjo clock, circa 1800, by one of the Willard brothers of Boston. Today, an Early-American room would seem strange indeed if not fully accessorized. Current devotees of seventeenth-century American furniture design, therefore, find it a good idea to accessorize their rooms with the mirrors, clocks ,and sconces that actually did not become readily available until the eighteenth century.

Colonial (1720–1789). Handsome and stately without being elaborate or overdone, American Colonial furniture has a wide appeal today. By modifying, simplifying, and substituting native cherry, pine, and maple for the English mahogany and walnut, Americans began turning out adaptations of Queen Anne chairs with cabriole legs and carved shell motifs, Chippendale highboys with curved pediments, Sheraton sideboards, and a profusion of pie-crust tables, wing chairs, and camel-back sofas. Some great original work was done, particularly the New England block-front style of cabinet that originated in Rhode Island—a

Post-Revolution
Federal

Fig. 60.

three-panel drawer front in which the center part was flat as a contrast for curving side sections.

Along with furniture, the wealthy found it necessary at first to import accessories from Europe or the Orient. Native craftsmen produced some fine clock designs. From 1700 on, American-made wall-hanging and shelf clocks were available in tasteful adaptations of Queen Anne, Sheraton, and other current styles. Other fine items were created in glass factories and in the shops of skilled silver, copper, and brass workers. Although mirrors were not generally available until later, there were some simplified Adam, Hepplewhite, and Queen Anne versions produced. Crystal, silver, or pewter chandeliers and lamps, bronze statuettes, pottery depicting colonial scenes, imported English china, and native paintings and engravings enriched the homes of those who could afford luxuries.

Post-Revolution Federal (*1789–1820*). The furniture produced in America after the Revolution is closely associated with Duncan Phyfe. He created free adaptations of English design with special emphasis on the work of Thomas Sheraton. During the latter part of his career he shifted to the French Empire style. His designs combined straight lines or modified curves with flared legs. Working in mahogany, he used carved ornamentation in classic motifs—swags, rosettes, and reeding. Among his best-known pieces are the Duncan Phyfe sofa, with outward-curving arms and flared legs, the round table with pedestal base, and the side chair with lyre back.

Toward the end of the Federal period, the feeling of national pride and patriotism that swept the country resulted in the adoption of the eagle as a symbol of American freedom. While there were no significant

Early-American

Fig. 61.

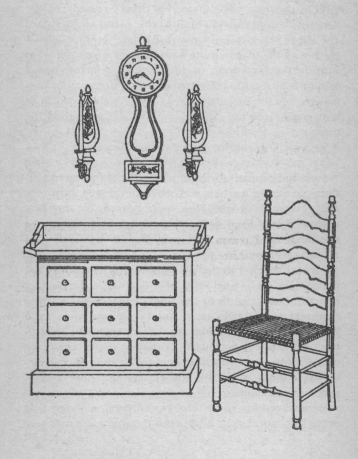

changes in the design of accessories, the clocks, mirrors, plaques, and sconces of the Sheraton-Hepplewhite influence suddenly blossomed forth with the new addition of a carved eagle.

The Provincial Styles

Like the expensive couturier dress created for the wealthy woman's way of life, the furniture designed for kings was not only expensive but impractical for the populace. In much the same way as a modern dress manufacturer takes an original couturier creation and adapts it for a moderate price, local French cabinetmakers of the seventeenth and eighteenth centuries borrowed from the court furniture and simplified the designs.

Provincial furniture originated in the outlying provinces surrounding the big cities. By using native woods and simple fabrics in place of the imported materials available to the court, they developed furniture and accessory designs that were compatible to their customer's mode of living. Generally scaled in size to suit the smaller room, provincial designs fit nicely into modern housing.

Most French Provincial furniture is based on the curved and feminine lines of Louis XV. There is a genuine rustic charm to the simpler pieces, such as the rush-seat ladderback chair and two-piece china cupboard that are much like the Early-American ladderback chair and pine hutch. Today an important piece of furniture in French Provincial styling is the armoire, once a substitute for closets and now a convenient high cabinet.

In addition to using clocks, mirrors, sconces, and other wall accessories that were modest adaptations of

French Provincial

Fig. 62.

those found in the palaces, the French middle class enriched their homes with objects made of pewter, china, porcelain, and pottery, some produced locally, and other pieces obtained from merchants who traded with the Far East.

Mediterranean (sixteenth to eighteenth century). The currently popular style referred to as Mediterranean is based on the heavy, solid construction and carved-wood surfaces of Italian and Spanish furniture and Moorish architecture. Chests and other cabinets feature paneled fronts in square or rectangular designs and metal ornamentation, as in the wrought-iron trestle-table bases.

Actually, the Mediterranean theme is more apparent in room backgrounds and accessories than in furniture. Rough-textured plaster walls, Moorish-patterned tile flooring, simulated in vinyl, beamed ceilings, doors rich with wood paneling, ornamental wrought-iron room dividers, gates, and window grilles—all of these Moorish-inspired details are part of Mediterranean. There are mirrors and clocks with wrought-ironlike frames in the lacy filigree patterns of Spain and Mexico, and sconces capturing the solid, substantial look of forged iron. In essence, the Mediterranean trend is important because it emphasizes a basic tenet of good decorating that can be applied to any style—it is the combination of accessories and architectural background details, rather than the furniture, that gives a room character and individuality.

Contemporary Styles

The revolution in architecture in the twentieth century has created the need for an entirely new type of

Mediterranean

Fig. 63.

furniture design—one that strips away the ginger-
bread of the past. After World War I, the Bauhaus
School was formed in Germany. It created the geometric school of modern, in which beauty stems from
the clean-lined simplicity of the design itself. Among
the most notable examples of this new approach to
beauty was the Barcelona group designed by Mies van
der Rohe and introduced at the Barcelona Fair in 1929.
Still manufactured in this country and considered a
classic of the modern school, Barcelona chairs and
tables rest on X-shaped curved cases of gleaming steel.
Seating pieces are grouped with exotic and colorful
plants, leaves, and flowers and mirrors that help reflect
the gleam of modern metals or the "wet" look of
shiny, vinyl-plastic fabrics. Personal collections—
ranging from family photographs to the potpourri of
hobbies or acquisitions from foreign travel—are emphasized as a means of self-expression in rooms filled
with machine-made furniture. Wall-hung furniture—
ranging from small curio cabinets and individual
shelves to all-encompassing built-in units—makes it
easy to display a number of personal possessions effectively without cluttering the room.

The simple T-squared table shown, known as the
Parsons table, was designed in the early '40's by stu-
dents at Parsons School of Design in New York. It
has become a contemporary classic and represents good
inexpensive design. The sculptured lines found in contemporary accessories soften the trim squared, contemporary upholstery that is so desired in today's
interiors.

Contemporary

Fig. 64.

GLOSSARY OF DECORATIVE MOTIFS

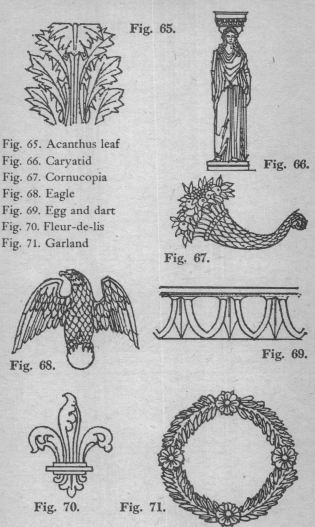

Fig. 65.

Fig. 65. Acanthus leaf
Fig. 66. Caryatid
Fig. 67. Cornucopia
Fig. 68. Eagle
Fig. 69. Egg and dart
Fig. 70. Fleur-de-lis
Fig. 71. Garland

Fig. 66.

Fig. 67.

Fig. 68.

Fig. 69.

Fig. 70.   Fig. 71.

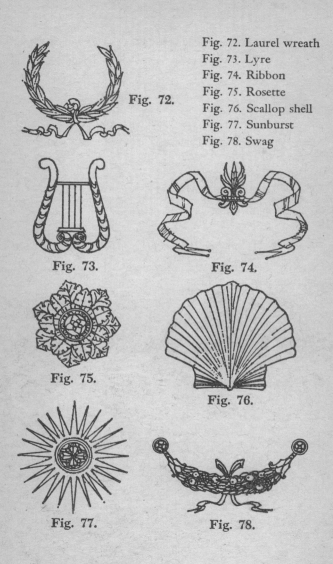

Fig. 72. Laurel wreath
Fig. 73. Lyre
Fig. 74. Ribbon
Fig. 75. Rosette
Fig. 76. Scallop shell
Fig. 77. Sunburst
Fig. 78. Swag

Fig. 72.

Fig. 73.

Fig. 74.

Fig. 75.

Fig. 76.

Fig. 77.

Fig. 78.

GLOSSARY

Accent: Certain element or elements used within an area that is different and contrasting to the overall tone; such as a contrasting color within a scheme.

Accessory: Any decorative object used within a room such as art objects, throw pillows, wall decorations, lamps that are separate from the major elements.

Antique: Painting, sculpture, furniture, and other objects produced over one hundred years ago. Prior to Feb. 1, 1967, the United States Customs law had set the date for antiques to have been produced prior to 1830.

Antiquing: A method of finishing to give an aged appearance. This is accomplished by hand rubbing, streaking, speckling, or

171

mottling paint, lacquer, or stain over a prime coat.

Baroque: A style or period developed in western Europe during the seventeenth century and first quarter of the eighteenth century. The design form is ornate and heavily ornamented.

Bevel: The edge of a mirror if cut at a slant to the main surface.

Bibelot: Any object that is usually small and decorative, having little value but still fun to own.

Cartouche: A convex surface, usually resembling a shield, surrounded with scrollwork or wreath design.

Cheval Glass: A full-length floor-standing mirror that can be tilted to desired adjustment.

Chinoiserie: A style of design and ornamentation popular in the eighteenth century in Europe, having patterns and motifs recognized as Chinese.

Collage: A technique of producing a work of art by pasting together various materials, such as: pieces of fabric, old photographs, and dried pressed leaves.

Collection: Any group of objects having a similar subject that is displayed together.

Console: A wall-hung shelf or table used in narrow spaces, usually has a curved front.

Convex Mirror: An outwardly rounded mirrored surface primarily used for decorative purposes.

Dado: A molding that's placed at a thirty-inch height from the floor to separate a wall into lower and upper sections. Also referred to as a chair rail.

Distressed: A term used to explain a type of finish applied to an object to give the appearance of age.

Eclectic: The art of combining furniture and accessories from various periods within the same decorative setting.

Etagere: A French open shelved pyramid-shaped cabinet used for the display of objects.

Etching: An impression which can be done in multiples taken from an etched metal plate. The picture produced is usually outlined sharply and clearly.

Faux Boix: A painted effect to resemble wood; usually the wood grain is exaggerated and made more definite.

Lavabo: A medieval hanging washbowl now used as a planter or decorative wall accessory.

Lithograph: A print produced in multiples from a flat specifically prepared stone, by taking ink impressions.

Matting: Flat edging material used for framing pictures, made from fabric or cardboard, which is then bordered by a wooden or metal frame.

Non-glare Glass: A special glass used for paintings, available in small sizes, which eliminates reflections of objects.

Objets d'Art: Any of the objects or accessories that have artistic and decorative value, usually expensive and rare.

Oil: A painting made on wood or canvas using only oil pigments. Oils are never covered with glass.

Pastel: The art of drawing with a crayon made from a chalklike stick. Drawings are usually soft and subdued.

Patina: The soft mellow finish which occurs on a surface through age and handling.

Pediment: A typically triangular pointed gable forming the cornice of classical doorways. Can be also found curved or split on mirrors with a finial or eagle placed in the center.

Pier Mirror: A tall elongated mirror, usually full length and framed, mounted in a narrow space.

Plate Glass: Glass formed by rolling hot glass into a plate which is then ground and polished.

Polychrome: Any object which has more than one color applied to its surface. Multicolored objects, such as painting the different color fruits in a fruit basket plaque.

Reeding: An elongated multiple half-round stem shape used as a carving design. A small convex molding; reeding is the reverse of fluting.

Reproduction: The copy or close reproducing of an original. Can be a multiple of any type of art as a version of an etching, lithograph, oil, water color, or pastel.

Rococo: A style of design and decoration that originated in France about 1725 and characteristically refined the Baroque lines. Delicate and romantic.

Sconce: A decorative wall fixture which holds candles or candelabra-type light bulbs, can be found designed in many different styles.

Scroll: An ornamental design resembling a repeated spiral. A roll of silk or paper with a painting on it that is displayed by hanging on a wall. Usually Chinese or Japanese.

Spindle: A long slim length of wood shaped and ornamented by turning on a lathe.

Stencil: To decorate or imprint with a design by painting through a cut-out pattern.

Tole: Tin or other metal which is shaped and then painted; finished item becomes a decorative object such as a chandelier or wall plaque.

Trumeau: Decorating the space over doors and mirrors usually with paintings or carved-wood reliefs. A trumeau mirror is one topped by a decorative panel found in Louis XV or Louis XVI styling, usually as paneling between two windows or over mantels during the eighteenth century.

Vitrine: A storage cabinet having clear glass doors and used to display objets d'art.

Watercolor: The art of painting whereby water is
mixed with the raw pigment instead
of oil; usually a light wash application
is used to create desired effect.

INDEX

Accessories, 15–21
    to add color, 17
    budget for, 105–106
    function of, 16–18
    furniture and, 41–43
    to give balance, 17–18
    lighting, 129–133
    period styles, 98–100, 137–167
    provincial, 140–141
    shopping for, 97–98
    traditional, 140, 142–162
Adam brothers, 142, 148–149
American styles, 99, 157–162
Antiques, 142
    reproductions, 142, 144
Armoires, 84, 162
Autumn decor, 102

Balance, 17, 27–29, 46
    accessories for, 17–18
    asymmetrical, 27
    decorating tricks, 58
    symmetrical, 27–29
Bathrooms, 92–93
Bauhaus School, 166

Bedrooms, 85–90
    lighting, 131
Bookshelves, 59, 61, 65
    built-in units, 43
    lighting, 130, 131, 133
    wall units, 59, 65
Breakfast rooms, 82
Budget for accessories, 105–106

Candelabra, 129
Chandeliers, 84, 131
Chippendale style, 142, 145, 146, 158
Christmas decor, 101
Clocks, 32, 82, 106, 158, 160
Collections of small items, 20, 26–27, 30, 131
Colonial style, 158–159
Color schemes, 17, 109–126
    accent colors, 111
    choosing, 110–112
    color intensity, 126
    complementary colors, 123
    cool and warm, 126
    creating illusions, 124–125

glossary of terms, 126
to minimize defects, 110
monochromatic, 122
primary colors, 122, 126
psychology of, 110
secondary, 122, 126
Contemporary styles, 56–57, 59, 64, 66, 166
accessories, 141
Contrast, use of, 17, 21
Cornices, 68, 131
Curio cabinets, 32, 121, 133

Decorating, 55–93
bathrooms, 92–93
bedrooms, 85–90
bookcase wall, 59, 61, 65
breakfast rooms, 82–84
dens and family rooms, 65–72
dining rooms, 81–84
fireplaces, 59, 62–63
kitchens, 91
living rooms, 59–64
mixing styles, 70, 138–139
Dens, decorating, 65–72
Dining areas, 32, 81–84
lighting, 129–133
Directoire style, 154–156

Early-American style, 99, 157–162
accessories, 140
Eighteenth-century English style, 99, 142–150
Empire style, 155–156, 160

Family rooms, 65–72
lighting, 130

Federal period, 99, 160–162
Fireplaces, 59, 62–63
Foyers, 20, 32
French provincial style, 81, 99, 162
accessories, 140–141
French traditional styles, 150–156
Furniture, coordinating accessories with, 41–43
motifs for, 138
styles, 142–167

Glossaries, 168–177
decorative motifs, 138
Grouping pictures, 20, 26–27, 30, 131

Hallways, 32
wall arrangements, 20
Handicrafts, 104–105
Hanging accessories, 41, 47–51
hooks and bolts, 50–51
types of walls, 50–51
Headboards, 43, 85
Hepplewhite style, 142, 146–148
Hobby collections, decorating with, 69, 103

Illusions, creating, 124–125
Interior designers, 98, 112, 139
Italian provincial, 164

Kitchens, 20, 91
lighting, 130–131

Lamps, 41
  area illuminated by, 130
  high-intensity, 131, 133
Lighting, 129–133
  bedrooms, 131
  bookshelves, 130, 131, 133
  dimmer switch, 129, 130, 131
  effect on color, 123–124
  levels of intensity, 130
  planning, 46, 129, 130
  special effects, 131–133
Living rooms, 56–64, 130
Louis XIV style, 150–151
Louis XV style, 142, 150–152, 162
Louis XVI style, 153, 154

Mantels, 21, 41–43, 148
Mediterranean provincial, 99–100, 164–165
Mirrors, 21, 30, 32, 106, 146
  hanging, 50
Mixing styles, 70, 138–139
Model-room settings, 98, 112, 139
Modern styles, 59, 141
Motifs, decorative, 138
  glossary of, 168–169

Paintings, 101, 106, 111
  lighting, 130
Phyfe, Duncan, 160–162
Pictures, 20, 106
  frames, 28, 41
  grouping, 26–27, 30
  hanging, 50–51
  matting for, 30
Planning wall arrangements, 25–51
  balance, 27–29

floor plans, 45–47
lighting, 46, 129, 130
pictures, 28–30
Planters, 20, 32, 90
Plants, 102–103
  lighting for, 133
  list of, 102–103
Playrooms, 71
Provincial styles, 56, 99–100, 104, 162–165
  accessories, 140–141
  French, 81, 99, 162
  Mediterranean, 99–100, 164–165

Queen Anne period, 142–146, 158

Sconces, 20, 32, 70, 84
Shelves, 32, 51
Sheraton style, 142, 146–148, 158, 160
Shopping for accessories, 97–106
Spanish style, 99, 164
Stairways, 20, 43
Styles of furniture, 142–167
  contemporary, 166–167
  mixing, 138–139
  provincial, 162–165
  traditional, 142–162
Summer decor, 101–102

Temporary homes, 106
Traditional styles, 142–144
  accessories, 140
  American, 157–162
  English, 142–150
  French, 150–156

Tridimensional objects, 20–21, 32, 41

van der Rohe, Mies, 166

Wall arrangements, 19–21
    creating, 18, 21
    planning, 25–51
Wallpaper, 83, 121, 144
Window treatments, 82–83

SYROCO

Syroco, founded in 1890 in Syracuse, N.Y., is the acknowledged style leader in the field of decorative accessories. With the largest design staff in the industry, the company continually designs accessories, tables and selects paintings that will complement current furniture styles as well as the great classical styles.

Each Syroco accessory begins with a hand-carved original. The carvings are done by a master craftsman in a wood especially selected for the nature of the object. Using the latest technology, accurate reproductions are made. An extremely important part of the Syroco product is the hand-finishing, the antiquing and polychroming that give Syroco accessories their rich look.

Syroco manufactures:

Syroco Wall Accessories—plaques, sconces, mirrors, planters, clocks

Syroco Art—original oils and reproductions in elegantly carved frames

Syroco Tables—an unusual series of cigarette, end and drum tables

Syroco Craft—paint-it-yourself wall accessory kits for adding a personal touch to the decor of any room

Syroco products are available in the picture and mirror, gift, clock, and adult hobby departments of most department stores, as well as furniture stores, gift shops, jewelry stores and craft stores.

Syroco is a member of the home furnishings division of Dart Industries Inc. (formerly Rexall).